Top Careers in Two Years

Communications and the Arts

Titles in the *Top Careers in Two Years* Series

Top Careers in Two Years

Communications and the Arts

By Claire Wyckoff

Ferguson Publishing
An imprint of Infobase Publishing

Top Careers in Two Years
Communications and the Arts

Ferguson
An imprint of Infobase Publishing
132 West 31st Street
New York, NY 10001

ISBN-13: 978-0-8160-6898-2
ISBN-10: 0-8160-6898-4

Library of Congress Cataloging-in-Publication Data

Top careers in two years.
    v. cm.
  Includes index.
  Contents: v. 1. Food, agriculture, and natural resources / by Scott Gillam — v. 2. Construction and trades / Deborah Porterfield — v. 3. Communications and the arts / Claire Wyckoff — v. 4. Business, finance, and government administration / Celia W. Seupal — v. 5. Education and social services / Jessica Cohn — v. 6. Health care, medicine, and science / Deborah Porterfield — v. 7. Hospitality, human services, and tourism / Rowan Riley — v. 8. Computers and information technology / Claire Wyckoff — v. 9. Public safety, law, and security / Lisa Cornelio, Gail Eisenberg — v. 10. Manufacturing and transportation — v. 11. Retail, marketing, and sales / Paul Stinson.
  ISBN-13: 978-0-8160-6896-8 (v. 1 : hc : alk. paper)
  ISBN-10: 0-8160-6896-8 (v. 1 : hc : alk. paper)
  ISBN-13: 978-0-8160-6897-5 (v. 2 : hc. : alk. paper)
  ISBN-10: 0-8160-6897-6 (v. 2 : hc. : alk. paper)
  ISBN-13: 978-0-8160-6898-2 (v. 3 : hc : alk. paper)
  ISBN-10: 0-8160-6898-4 (v. 3 : hc : alk. paper)
  ISBN-13: 978-0-8160-6899-9 (v. 4 : hc : alk. paper)
  ISBN-10: 0-8160-6899-2 (v. 4 : hc : alk. paper)
  ISBN-13: 978-0-8160-6900-2 (v. 5 : hc : alk. paper)
  ISBN-10: 0-8160-6900-X (v. 5 : hc : alk. paper)
  ISBN-13: 978-0-8160-6901-9 (v. 6 : hc : alk. paper)
  ISBN-10: 0-8160-6901-8 (v. 6 : hc : alk. paper)
  ISBN-13: 978-0-8160-6902-6 (v. 7 : hc : alk. paper)
  ISBN-10: 0-8160-6902-6 (v. 7 : hc : alk. paper)
  ISBN-13: 978-0-8160-6903-3 (v. 8 : hc : alk. paper)
  ISBN-10: 0-8160-6903-4 (v. 8 : hc : alk. paper)
  ISBN-13: 978-0-8160-6904-0 (v. 9 : hc : alk. paper)
  ISBN-10: 0-8160-6904-2 (v. 9 : hc : alk. paper)
  ISBN-13: 978-0-8160-6905-7 (v. 10 : hc : alk. paper)
  ISBN-10: 0-8160-6905-0 (v. 10 : hc : alk. paper)
  ISBN-13: 978-0-8160-6906-4 (v. 11 : hc : alk. paper)
  ISBN-10: 0-8160-6906-9 (v. 11 : hc : alk. paper)
  1. Vocational guidance—United States. 2. Occupations—United States. 3. Professions—United States.
  HF5382.5.U5T677 2007
  331.7020973—dc22

                                                                    2006028638

Produced by Print Matters, Inc.
Text design by A Good Thing, Inc.
Cover design by Salvatore Luongo

Printed in the United States of America

MP PMI 10 9 8 7 6 5 4 3 2 1

This book is printed on acid-free paper.

Contents

Contents

How to Use This Book

This book, part of the *Top Careers in Two Years* series, highlights in-demand careers for readers considering a two-year degree program—either straight out of high school or after working a job that does not require advanced education. The focus throughout is on the fastest-growing jobs with the best potential for advancement in the field. Readers learn about future prospects while discovering jobs they may never have heard of.

An associate's degree can be a powerful tool in launching a career. This book tells you how to use it to your advantage, explore job opportunities, and find local degree programs that meet your needs.

Each chapter provides the essential information needed to find not just a job but a career that fits your particular skills and interests. All chapters include the following features:

- ☞ "Vital Statistics" provides crucial information at a glance, such as salary range, employment prospects, education or training needed, and work environment.

- ☞ Discussion of salary and wages notes hourly versus salaried situations as well as potential benefits. Salary ranges take into account regional differences across the United States.

- ☞ "Keys to Success" is a checklist of personal skills and interests needed to thrive in the career.

- ☞ "A Typical Day at Work" describes what to expect at a typical day on the job.

- ☞ "Two-Year Training" lays out the value of an associate's degree for that career and what you can expect to learn.

- ☞ "What to Look For in a School" provides questions to ask and factors to keep in mind when selecting a two-year program.

- ☞ "The Future" discusses prospects for the career going forward.

- ☞ "Interview with a Professional" presents firsthand information from someone working in the field.

ᴥ "Job Seeking Tips" offers suggestions on how to meet and work with people in the field, including how to get an internship or apprenticeship.

ᴥ "Career Connections" lists Web addresses of trade organizations providing more information about the career.

ᴥ "Associate's Degree Programs" provides a sampling of some of the better-known two-year schools.

ᴥ "Financial Aid" provides career-specific resources for financial aid.

ᴥ "Related Careers" lists similar related careers to consider.

In addition to a handy comprehensive index, the back of the book features two appendices providing invaluable information on job hunting and financial aid. Appendix A, Tools for Career Success, provides general tips on interviewing either for a job or two-year program, constructing a strong résumé, and gathering professional references. Appendix B, Financial Aid, introduces the process of applying for aid and includes information about potential sources of aid, who qualifies, how to prepare an application, and much more.

Acknowledgments

My thanks to the many faculty and other staff at all the two-year schools who helped with the research for this book. Although numerous individuals and institutions assisted in its preparation, certain individuals stand out for their extraordinary assistance. They include:

For Music—Vance Larsen, Snow Community College
For Interior Design—Laurie White, Tidewater Community College,
For Audio Engineering—Rick Shriver, University of Ohio
For Broadcast Engineering—Steve Keeler, Cayuga Community College
For Dance—Elaine Mowining, Northern Essex Community College
For Desktop Publishing—Morgan Tyree, Northwest Community College
For Fashion Design—Ruth Carlson, West Valley Community College
For Library Technology—Brian Kleeman, College of Dupage
For Lighting Technology—Jim Moody, City College of Los Angeles
For Photography—Tom Turner, Pacific Union College
For Video Technology—Luwin Sanchez, Art Institute of Florida

Special thanks also to Mary C. Taylor of the Library & Information Technology Association (LITA) and Jan Timpano at the National Association of Schools of Music (NASM).

Introduction

Have you ever thought about how much time you spend talking with friends and family, listening to the radio, watching TV, and surfing the Web? If you add it all up, you'll quickly realize that communication is the most important activity in your day. Good communication is what helps you influence others, build relationships, and make sense of the world around you.

Just as communication is important to you, it is critical to the health of communities. In fact it is the very foundation of society. Without it, we could not help and entertain each other, share information, or build networks.

Thanks to technology, our ability to communicate has evolved beyond the mere interpersonal level. We send words, sounds, images, and moving pictures over the air (radio/telephone/television/microwaves), on hard copy through printed material, over the Internet with cables and airwaves, and out into space and back (satellites).

People pursue communications and arts careers for a variety of reasons. However, two stand out. One is a strong, natural aptitude in the arts (e.g., music and dance). The other is an interest in the technical side of getting arts and information to the public (e.g., broadcast engineering and desktop publishing). For individuals in either category, obtaining an associate's degree from a two-year program may provide exactly the right academic foundation for their professional development.

Benefits of an Associate's Degree

While those with artistic talent may be tempted to bypass study beyond the high school level, the courses required for a two-year degree give many of the basic skills that today's digitized world demands. Community colleges, trade schools, vocational schools, art institutes, and other two-year schools all have the excellent training programs to reach your careers goals in communications and the arts. Some four-year colleges even offer two-year programs.

The majority of students who earn associate's degrees, though, do so at community colleges. Today around six million students attend approximately 1,200 public and independent community colleges. Besides providing strong guidance and technical training, community colleges offer many other advantages. Their admission requirements are often less challenging than those of four-year institutions. They are flexible and affordable. They provide a caring environment, whose faculty are known for meeting students' individual needs—regardless of age, gender, race, current job status, or previous education. They provide opportunities for hands-on experience.

An attractive feature of two-year colleges is that admission is not highly competitive. Students are admitted from a wide range of academic backgrounds. So someone who performed below average in high school can excel at a two-year school if he or she puts time and energy into study.

The difference in the cost of a two-year education is also significant. Recent statistics from the College Board reported the annual cost at a public two-year institution averaging $2,191, which compared very favorably to the average $21,235 annual tuition and fees at a four-year private college.

As far as financial aid is concerned, there is plenty of funding available to those attending trade, technical, vocational, two-year, and career colleges. The College Board's latest statistics show those who attend two-year public colleges are receiving grant aid that averages about $2,300. The U.S. Department of Education provides a list of institutions at http://www.ope.ed.gov/accreditation/index.asp that are accredited to offer federal financing. For more financial aid information, check out Appendix B.

Since community colleges are found in every region of the United States, most students are enrolled locally. Some are now even able to get instruction at home through their regional cable TV or Internet service. This means they can choose to save money by living at home and have a level of flexibility that makes it easy to work while going to school. Still, those looking for the more traditional college experience will find that at least 20 percent of two-year colleges provide housing, cafeterias, sports, clubs, and the same bustling social scene that many four-year schools boast.

The profiles of community college faculty also reveal that many hold jobs in the career fields in which they teach. As a result, students in these programs get realistic career guidance. They are also likely to spend a lot of their time getting "hands-on" experience. They either work on-site at actual businesses or they perform practical exercises in the classroom that give them real-world experience. For example, students at the Art Institute of Pittsburgh helped design a bicycle that scientists could use in Antarctica—drawing up blueprints and creating a prototype. Especially for those entering the field of communications, this real-world experience is often a prerequisite for landing an entry-level position, and many internships and apprenticeships lead directly to full-time employment.

This experience is invaluable to anyone who decides to enter a communications-related career. As the descriptions in this book reveal, these are very competitive fields, and this real-world experience may make the difference in landing an entry-level job. For some an internship itself may lead to a full-time job; for others it provides the practical know-how that distinguishes them from other job applicants.

Finally, anyone who wants a meaningful career in communications and the arts should be aware of the income boost that a two-year degree provides. Compared to those who hold only a high school degree, holders of associate's degrees earn more money ($2,000–$6,000 a year more on average) and face a much lower rate of unemployment. In 2001 the unemployment rate was more than 30 percent lower for associate's degree holders compared with high school graduates. Equally significant, workers with an associate's degree averaged $128 a week more than high school graduates in 2001, according to the Bureau of Labor Statistics (BLS). Also, consider that 43 percent of four-year college graduates are underemployed: This means that some may be taking jobs at fast-food chains, even though they spent $100,000 to get a bachelor's degree in philosophy. Plus, the world needs more workers with hands-on skills. There's a shortage of people with technical training, including those trained at the two-year level.

These are among the reasons that many successful people working in communications and arts today chose to get associate's degrees. Some of the notables who graduated from two-year programs include:

William Bresnan
President and CEO
Bresnan Communications

Jerry Crutchfield
President
MCA Publishing

Gerald Gordon
President and CEO
SunMedia Corporation

Carol Guzy
News Photographer
The Washington Post

Michael Johnson
President and Managing Director
Walt Disney Int'l. Asia
Buena Vista Home Video, Walt Disney

Andrew Lock
Owner
andyCam Video Production Team

Keith Philpott
Professional Photographer
Keith Philpott Photography

Chuck Scarborough
Anchor and Correspondent
NBC, Channel 4 (WNBC)

Billy Dean
Country music performer

Valerio Azzoli
Co-Chair and Co-CEO
Atlantic Recording Corp.

John Walsh
Host
America's Most Wanted
Fox Television Station, Inc.

Today's two-year curricula are as diverse as the many different aspects of communications these careers address. No matter what aspect of communications and the arts interests you, you'll find excellent two-year programs to prepare you for them. If working behind the scenes in a television or radio station sounds appealing, training to become a video editor, or radio or television broadcast technician are good choices. These workers run soundboards, editing machinery, and other broadcast equipment, and they often learn how by earning an associate's degree. Several degrees are available for artistic types. Desktop publishing, multimedia, and graphic arts are the fastest growing art-related degrees. Graduates work as artists, Web masters, and animators.

Interior design is another popular artistic major. Entry-level positions in industrial design, fashion design, and set design are also available to workers with associate's degrees.

Marketplace

While communications remains a highly competitive field, the number of opportunities has multiplied significantly, thanks to the growth of new media. In 2004 broadcast, audio, and sound engineering technicians and radio operators held about 93,000 jobs. Their employment was distributed among the following detailed occupations:

Audio and video equipment technicians	42,000
Broadcast technicians	35,000
Sound engineering technicians	13,000
Radio operators	3,000

In the video field, television, video, and motion picture camera operators held about 28,000 jobs, and film and video editors held about 20,000 jobs. Photographers held about 129,000 jobs.

Musicians, singers, and related workers held about 249,000 jobs. Around 40 percent worked part time; almost half were self-employed. Many found jobs in cities in which entertainment and recording activities are concentrated, such as New York, Los Angeles, Las Vegas, Chicago, and Nashville. Professional dancers and choreographers held about 37,000 jobs

Recent figures for designers were comparable. In 2004 they held about 556,000 jobs (and approximately one-third were self-employed). Employment was distributed as follows:

Graphic designers	228,000
Floral designers	98,000
Merchandise displayers and window trimmers	86,000
Interior designers	65,000
Commercial and industrial designers	49,000
Fashion designers	17,000
Set and exhibit designers	13,000

Library technicians held about 109,000 jobs in 2004.

Equally important to those starting out now is that communications will continue to be a booming field. Two industries in particular—cable and the Internet—depend on people who are trained in communications technologies and provide many opportunities for them. In the 10-year period beginning in 2004, the Bureau of Labor Statistics estimates employment in the cable and other subscription businesses will grow from 85,600 to 125,000 jobs—a very healthy 46 percent. Just behind this are jobs for independents, which the Bureau of Labor Statistics projects will grow from 41,900 to 60,800, or 45 percent. For the Internet publishing and broadcasting fields, the comparable figures are 31,300 to 44,900, or 43 percent. Another way of stating these figures is that 72,500 new jobs will become available in these industries in the next 10 years.

Are Communications and the Arts for You?

If you are considering a career in communications and the arts, it's important to check out the kinds of skills and aptitudes that are needed for success in these fields.

Traits

Certainly, creativity would have to be at the top of the list. Nearly every career in communications and the arts—from jazz musician to lighting technician—requires imagination. Communications workers must have the ability to see the world in a somewhat unique way—bringing their own interpretations to the world around them.

The ability to work independently is also important. As the descriptions in this book illustrate, many of the dedicated workers in these fields are self-employed. They know how to survive on their own, often operating their work lives like a small business—paying all their own taxes, scheduling their work, paying for their own insurance, etc. The self-employed make prompt decisions, are good organizers, and manage their finances well.

For many communications and arts professionals, good health and robust physical condition are priorities. The work of lighting technicians, for example, requires stamina because they are expected to move heavy equipment around. They also mount lights in high places, so they can't suffer from a fear of heights! Photographers also carry heavy equipment, and they may be faced with exposure to harsh climates and bad weather conditions. Dancers' bodies are their livelihoods, and they must maintain them well. Most dancers have to stop or cut back on performing as they reach their forties because their bodies can't sustain the stress. Even so, dance teachers practice several hours every day.

Some of the physical aptitudes are very specific. Dancers need to be well coordinated and agile. Musicians depend on manual dexterity. Broadcast engineers also rely on their hands to mend wires and repair audio equipment. Keen eyesight is important to video editors as well as photographers.

Skills and Applications

Most successful communications and arts workers are good team players. While many of their jobs require them to work independently, the projects they are assigned to involve many different skills. In most instances, it's very important for them to interact well with a lot of people and communicate clearly; for instance, consider fashion designers. After a fashion designer creates a sketch, she or he may refine it in a digital file, or (just as likely) ask an assistant to do it. Fashion designers must speak with contacts at fabric houses to find just the right materials; and then they have to instruct the pattern makers and seamstresses on how to construct their designs correctly.

Computer savvy and knowledge of digital technologies are also vital in today's communications and arts careers. Fashion designers use specialized software programs to finish their patterns; interior designers use programs to create their plans; broadcast engineers, audio technicians, and video editors apply specific software programs to create the effects they want. Many photographers and videographers no longer use film; they capture their images digitally so they can be manipulated and reproduced via computer.

In the chapters that follow, you'll read about 12 career paths in the communications field that two-year programs can prepare you for. Of course, there are many more; your guidance counselor probably can tell you how to find out more about them.

Animator

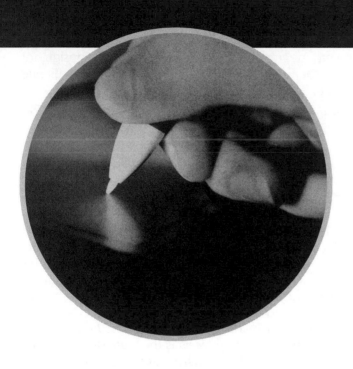

Vital Statistics

Salary: Animators have a median annual salary of about $50,000, according to 2006 data from the U.S. Bureau of Labor Statistics. Enry-level workers earn about $30,000 a year.

Employment: The field is growing as fast as the average of other occupations, with opportunities increasing in Web, cable TV, and CD-ROM producion.

Education: A two-year degree in animation, multimedia design, or graphic design is necessary. Prerequisites include basic art courses and some computer training. Some experience with film is helpful.

Work Environment: In-home studios or offices equipped with easels, bright lights, drawing supplies, and computers.

Say goodbye to Mickey Mouse and Bambi. A few years ago, the Disney Corporation closed all of its studios that created hand-drawn animation to focus on computer animation. The change had been gradually happening over the past decade, but when Disney threw out the hand-drawn mouse for the hand-held mouse and computer screen, it was a real sign that the world of animation had changed—especially in film.

Computer-animated movies like *The Incredibles, Monsters Inc., Toy Story,* and *Shrek* have been blockbusters. *Saving Nemo* is the highest-earning animated feature of all time and one of the highest grossing films in Hollywood history. Proving less popular have been recent hand-drawn animated features such as *Brother Bear, Treasure Planet,* and *Atlantis.*

The job of any animator is to bring images to life by stringing them together in a series so they appear to move when shown in rapid succession. Computer animation makes the process less time consuming and less costly, and it has been generating more profit for the studios that produce animated features. Simply put, there is a huge demand for computer animation, so there is a huge demand for computer animators.

You'll even find these high-tech techniques incorporated in live-action films. Special effects in movies like *The Matrix* and *Titanic* depend on computer animation technology. Electronic gaming is another area that has grown more sophisticated in its use on computer animation. The three-dimensional (3-D) images and landscapes in Microsoft Xbox and Nintendo games can be very detailed, and the motion is now quite fluid and realistic.

So are old-fashioned pen-and-pencil drawings gone forever? Not quite. On TV, hand-drawn cartoons still attract a large audience, and they're not just for kids any more. Shows like *The Simpsons, Family Guy,* and *South Park* have shown that cartoons definitely have an adult audience (at least for those who are teenagers at heart).

Whether the animation is a high-speed car chase on a video game or Homer Simpson chasing his son Bart, the work requires meticulous planning. Each individual frame of any animation has to be planned, and a full-length animated film requires hundreds of thousands of frames and teams of artists. Although computers have made the work easier, you don't just push a button and out pops the final product. "Computers don't create computer animation any more than a pencil would create a drawing," says John Lasseter, director of creative development at Pixar.

For each animated project, artists create characters, scripts, and storyboards. Computer animators develop models of their characters, often using points and lines connected together and situated in a 3-D virtual space. To flesh out their basic models, they use techniques such as shading and rendering (smoothing out the geometric construction to produce realistic shape, light, and shadows). The computer cuts down on the actual animation work, nevertheless. While a stop-motion or cel (for *celluloid*) animator creates 24 frames for one second of film, the computer animator can create only three or four key frames and the computer fills in the *inbetween* frames.

"Computer animators don't just have a fancy electric pencil—you have to know how to draw."
—Frank Gladstone, manager of
animation training for Disney

On the Job

A starting place for many animators has been in the *inbetween department.* An *inbetween* is one of the transition drawings between two *extreme* drawings. Extremes are called the animator's *key* drawings and demonstrate the essence of an animated action. The inbetweens fill in the action between these key drawings (still retaining their essence, yet never distracting from them). New animators need to learn to work in a team and imitate the animator's drawings and line quality.

New animators also may lend a hand creating storyboards. Storyboards visually outline the story of a movie—they are panels that depict the action and staging of the film's script. The storyboard is really the first step in the animation process. Layout is another area in which beginners may lend a hand. Layout is the background design for animation. Layout artists render pencil background drawings for each production scene. They often research the relevant geography or time period to make sure things are accurate in the story. Clean-up artists go over the work and make sure everything is neat, colors match, and details are the same from frame to frame.

No matter what the job, animators spend much of their time working alone. This may be because almost half of all artists work for themselves, according to the Bureau of Labor Statistics. Still teamwork is essential for big animated projects and professionals in the field often have to work as a team to plan and coordinate their efforts. Animators have to be flexible, often putting in long hours to meet project deadlines. Often, animators work on a project-by-project basis, so when a job ends, they may find themselves out of work and looking for their next gig. Because opportunities are most available in big cities, animators have to be ready to live in New York, Los Angeles, or Chicago. Keep in mind too that this is a very creative industry, so be ready to work with a lot of quirky, creative people.

Keys to Success

To be a successful animator, you should have strong
- art skills
- communication skills
- computer know-how
- solitary work habits
- attention to detail
- fine motor skills
- self-starter abilities

Do You Have What It Takes?

Students interested in animation should have a passion for art and drawing and a natural artistic talent. If you're the type of person who has spent years doodling or creating cartoon characters, this may be a perfect career option for you. While in high school, budding animators can build their skills by taking as many art classes as possible. Courses in film and acting can also help because a lead animator who directs a film works with real actors who provide the voices—and they have to understand how to create dramatic story lines. High school students should study the animated films they like carefully, taking notes about the voices, plot, music, and other details.

A Typical Day at Work

A typical day for an animator can begin with a review of *dailies*, which are filmed sections of animation from the previous days. At these meetings, animators, directors, and editors gather to discuss if the animation has been done properly or needs improvement. Then animators usually go back to the drawing board, working alone and together to bring the script to life. If working on 3-D computer animation, an artist may spend the bulk of the day making *map* paintings of 3-D images to use as scene backgrounds. These computer paintings are usually of nature—snow, rain, clouds, etc. Once they are created, they save other artists time because they don't have to recreate backgrounds in every frame, they simply pop the map paintings into the background. Other artists focus on clean-up, inbetween frames, or developing the storyboards that outline the main action of a film. At the end of the day, supervisors go to each animator's office to review their work one more time. This is often called a *walkthru*.

How to Break In

While working on an associate's degree, young animators must develop a portfolio of work that demonstrates their creativity and variety of talents. Typically, associate's degree students have to create a demo reel, a film showing they can create a title sequence, simple animation, a scene with camera movement, and other basic techniques. Two-year schools stress hands-on opportunities and often provide internships at animation studios that can give artists the experience they need to advance. Many major corporations offer internships to two-year students, including Disney, DreamWorks, SKG, Nickelodeon Pixar, Microsoft, Sony Image Works, and Warner Bros.

Two-Year Training

Two-year associate's degree programs in animation hone skills that are specifically needed to begin a career and land an entry-level job. Typical courses are animation programming, audio for animation, character development, cinematography, the art of the narrative, principles of 3-D modeling, and camera techniques. Many two-year schools have computer animation labs in which students get hands-on experience using the latest hardware and software. Basic art courses such as life drawing are essential as well. Animators need to study the fine arts—not only drawing, but also sculpting and painting. Acting and directing skills can help since creating animation is similar to creating a live-action movie in many ways. It helps to have a broad base of knowledge to draw on—so courses in history, geography, and life sciences can be very helpful.

What to Look For in a School

Breaking into the business depends a lot on the two-year school you pick. Be sure to ask these questions:

☞ Will the school teach me how to draw and tell a story?

☞ Will I learn all the technical skills needed to master computer animation?

☞ What internships are available and what is the school's job placement rate?

☞ Does the school specialize in areas of animation that interest me?

☞ What are the professors' credentials? Have they worked in the industry? How available are professors outside of the classroom?

☞ What are the labs like and do they have the latest equipment? Check to make sure you will be trained using the four main software packages: Alias Power Animator/Maya, Kinetix 3D Studio Max, SoftImage, and Lightwave.

The Future

Opportunities in animation go well beyond television and movies. Web sites now use flash animation to make splashier pages, medical institutions turn to animation for instructional purposes, the aerospace industry has used animation to train its new pilots, and scientists rely on animation to demonstrate events such as the course of a tsunami. A new animation career is that of forensic animator. These specialists recreate events related to court cases—from a traffic accident or to the spatial relationships in a crime. As animation is used in more and more industries, those starting out will find an increasing range of employment possibilities.

Job Seeking Tips

Follow these specific tips for animators and then turn to Appendix A for help with résumés and interviewing.

✔ Build a portfolio that shows a range of your styles and talents.

✔ Decide what you're interested in and seek relevant experience.

✔ Talk to the career placement office.

✔ Try to gain an internship at an animation studio that produces work that you admire.

Interview with a Professional:
Q&A

Derek Drymon

Creative director andsupervising producer on
Nickelodeon's *SpongeBob Squarepants*

Q: *How did you get started?*

A: I studied at the School of Visual Arts in New York and it was great because I had nothing else to do but concentrate on my art. Then I interned at Disney in Orlando. After working there with some of the best in the business, I found a job at Nickelodeon as a clean-up artist.

Q: *What's a typical day like?*

A: I sit down with the writers to come up with story ideas and give notes on the completed scripts. Scripts then go to storyboard where all the scenes are drawn in television format. I also approve characters, background, and prop designs. Before the episode can be sent overseas for the actual animation, the voices have to be recorded. I meet with the casting director to approve voice actors. My work isn't completed on an episode until it comes back from animation (up to a 6-month process) and film, sound effects, and music editing is finished.

Q: *What's your advice for those starting a career?*

A: Getting the experience in an animation studio is crucial. You really have to see in person how an animation team works.

Q: *What's the best part of being an animator?*

A: Being able to create and work with creative people is a blast. Having characters come to life from your imagination is incredible and I can't believe I get paid to do this work.

Did You Know?

TV producers love animated series because they are relatively inexpensive. Compared to hit comedy series, which costs $5–6 million per episode to produce, an animated series only costs about $2 million per episode.

Career Connections

For more information contact the following organizations:

Animation Arena http://www.animationarena.com

Animation World News http://www.awn.com

Animation School Review http://www.animationschoolreview.com

SIGGRAPH (Special Interest Group on Computer Graphics and Interactive Techniques) http://www.siggraph.org

Don Bluth Studios
Don Bluth has created major animated features in the last 25 years and this Web site gives very detailed, step-by-step view of the animation process and the roles involved.   http://www.donbluth.com

Associate's Degree Programs

Here are a few schools offering quality animation programs:

The Art Institutes (AI), Pittsburgh, Pennsylvania

Brooks College, Long Beach, California

Westwood College, 18 campuses and online

Platt College, San Diego, California

Digital Media Arts College, online

IIT Tech, more than 85 locations nationwide

Financial Aid

Here are two animation-related scholarships. Turn to Appendix B for more on financial aid for two-year students.

Worldstudio AIGA Scholarships http://www.worldstudio.org

The Art Institute of California San Francisco animation scholarships. Call 888-493-3261.

Related Careers

Graphic designer, art director, game designer, and computer graphics programmer.

Library Technician

Vital Statistics

Salary: On average, library technicians earn about $24,900. Salaries start at $14,760 and can go as high as $41,000 according to 2006 figures from the U.S. Bureau of Labor Statistics.

Employment: Tight budgets are limiting the number of jobs in this field. However, library support staff—especially if they have strong computer and research skills—are in demand in government agencies, corporations, law firms, advertising agencies, museums, medical centers, research laboratories, and other nonprofits. Growth overall in the number of library technicians is expected to keep pace with the average for all occupations.

Education: Earning a library technical assistant (LTA) degree takes about 65 hours of courses, including 26 hours of study in library and information resource management. Students may design programs with special concentrations in online and electronic information, library information systems, customer service, book and print materials, or media and multimedia. They also may be required to complete and internship.

Work Environment: Most techs work in the quiet, orderly atmosphere of a library. Techs, or LTs as they are called sometimes, probably spend a lot of time doing research or other computer-based tasks or assist visitors to the library. However, nearly half of all LTs work for public library systems, where they are often expected to staff bookmobiles, traveling around their communities in vans.

If you think library technicians just shelve books, think again. Today's library technicians often work with complex computer systems. Some make vital contributions to cutting-edge research, while others help people with disabilities and senior citizens by taking responsibility for their community's bookmobiles. Moreover, library technicians, or LTs, don't just work in public libraries these days; they also staff libraries in universities, major corporations (especially in the pharmaceutical, health care, and biotech fields), museums, and nonprofits involved in complex research projects. Potential employers range from the Ford Foundation and the pharmaceutical company Pfizer to the Academy of Motion Picture Arts and Sciences and the Museum of Modern Art in New York City.

While technicians assist librarians, they are expected to work independently. The primary jobs of the LT are to order, prepare, and organize new materials the library decides to acquire and to help users find information. Tasks range from preparing invoices, cataloging and coding library materials, and retrieving information from computer databases, to supervising other support staff. In smaller libraries, library technicians have varied responsibilities, while in larger libraries technicians usually specialize in particular functions.

The increasing popularity of obtaining information from computerized systems means that technicians now handle many technical services that librarians used to perform. These include entering catalog information into the library's computer and customizing databases. Many libraries also now offer self-service registration and circulation areas with computers, decreasing the time library technicians spend manually recording and inputting records.

As libraries continue to expand their use of new technologies—such as CD-ROM, the Internet, virtual libraries, and automated databases—the duties of library technicians will evolve accordingly. For example, library technicians are now responsible for instructing users in how to use computer systems to access data. Some library technicians also operate and maintain audiovisual equipment, such as projectors, tape and CD players, and DVD and videocassette players, and assist users with microfilm or microfiche readers.

Technicians who work in public libraries may be expected to drive bookmobiles that take library services out into the community. Bookmobile operators work with personal computers and CD-ROM systems linked to the library's main system. The LTs use these to locate and reserve books quickly. Some bookmobiles also offer users Internet access.

Technicians may take requests for special items from the main library and arrange for the materials to be mailed or delivered to users during the next scheduled visit. They also help plan programs sponsored by the library, such as author readings, children's story hours, reader advisory programs, book sales, or other outreach efforts.

A lot of the job is about organization. Technicians keep records on circulation and the number of patrons served, the materials lent out, and the amount of fines collected. If the library has limited funding, LTs may have to take on maintenance duties as well, from fixing photocopiers to servicing the library vehicles.

On the Job

As information specialists, librarians spend a lot of their time answering questions and providing assistance to library users. Some also may be expected to engage in a great deal of physical activity—lifting and carrying books, climbing ladders to reach high stacks, and bending to shelve books on bottom shelves. Often the physical work is a welcome break from sitting behind a desk or at a computer terminal for long periods preparing library materials. At other times, techs get creative, designing posters, bulletin boards, and displays.

Although they work independently, technicians start out working under the supervision of a librarian. With experience, they usually take on more responsibilities. Techs in public and college libraries often start at the circulation desk, checking books in and out; but over time, they take on more sophisticated duties, such as storing and verifying information on computers. With experience, they may tackle budget and personnel matters. Some LTs advance to supervisory positions in which they are in charge of the day-to-day operation of their departments.

> ## "Outside of a dog, a book is a man's best friend. Inside of a dog, it's too dark to read."
> —Groucho Marx, humorist

 ## Keys to Success

For success as a library technician, you should have

- a methodical approach to work
- good organizational and time management skills
- interpersonal skills
- a service orientation
- good speaking and listening skills
- strong computer training
- an ability to teach others

Do You Have What It Takes?

If you enjoy working with people and books, and also like to operate computers, the job of library technician could be an excellent fit. While some of the duties you may be asked to perform—like calculating circulation statistics—can be repetitive and boring, computer searches using library networks and other systems can be very interesting and challenging.

Ideal library technicians are organized and efficient, excited about learning new things, and eager to help others. In high school, they may have enjoyed surfing the Web and showing their buddies what they found. To channel this aptitude, techs might start by studying software programs that support Internet research. Knowledge of database programs can be helpful as well.

A Typical Day at Work

A typical day for library technicians varies a lot depending on the kind of library in which they work. A corporate library tech may focus on intensive research. A tech at a pharmaceutical firm may have to find out all the studies that were performed with a possible cancer-inhibiting drug, which involves conducting computer searches, compiling bibliographies, and preparing abstracts of books and articles on the subject.

In school libraries, technicians assist and teach students to use the library and media center. They also may help students with special assignments, locate instructional materials for teachers, and design displays for the library.

The technicians who operate bookmobiles drive to designated sites on a regular schedule, frequently stopping at shopping centers, apartment complexes, schools, and nursing homes. Because library technicians who operate bookmobiles often interact with people of limited mobility, they may need to rely on sensitive interpersonal skills. Bookmobile technicians may assist handicapped or elderly patrons to the bookmobile or clear snow from the sidewalk to ease their passage. They may even visit hospitals or nursing homes to deliver books to bedridden patrons. Depending on local conditions, the technicians may operate a bookmobile alone or be accompanied by another library employee.

Part-time hours are more common for library technicians than people with other jobs. Usually, however, library technicians in public libraries work regular business hours, as well as weekends, evenings, and some holidays. This schedule also applies to technicians in college and university (academic) libraries. Library technicians in special libraries are expected to work normal business hours, and they often put in overtime as well. Library technicians who drive bookmobiles report in as needed, usually depending on the size of the community being served. Some bookmobiles operate in the evenings and weekends, to give patrons as much access to the library as possible. Like teachers, school librarians and library technicians typically have time off during the summer when facilities are closed.

How to Break In

An associate's degree, combined with previous library experience, will make you employable. Many people volunteer at libraries to explore the job, gain vital skills, and possibly land an entry-level position. Since library budgets have been under pressure in recent years, librarians often welcome this help. Whether working at the library or just visiting, you should also be sure to make time to observe librarians at work and also explore how the library organizes information.

Joining library organizations can boost your employment search. The Council on Library Technicians (COLT) is the oldest support staff organization that represents technicians on a national level, but more organizations are adding programs. Regionally, library consortiums offer affordable training sessions in all types of library skills.

Proof of computer skills may give you an advantage over other applicants for the job. To improve your communications skills, you might consider adding psychology to your mix of courses.

Two-Year Training

Training requirements for library technicians vary widely. While some employers hire individuals with work experience or other training, most employers prefer to hire technicians who have an associate's degree or some other postsecondary training. An associate's degree or certificate program includes both liberal arts and library-related study. Students learn about library and media organization and operation, as well as how to order, process, catalog, locate, and circulate library materials and work with library automation. Given the rapid spread of automation in libraries, computer skills are essential: knowledge of databases, library automation systems, online library systems, online public access systems, and circulation systems are particularly valuable. Many bookmobile drivers must obtain a commercial driver's license as well.

What to Look For in a School

Be sure to ask these questions:

☞ Does the school issue credentials in the field?

☞ Is its program affordable for you?

☞ Is it close to home and/or work (if you are attending part time)?

☞ Are some courses offered online?

☞ Is an internship required to obtain a degree?

☞ Does the school offer a placement service for library technicians?

The Future

Although competition for jobs as library technicians is keen, education, training, and experience can lead to a rewarding career. For some, a job as a library technician can even lead to becoming a librarian.

Growth in the number of professionals and other workers who use special libraries should result in good job opportunities for library technicians in those settings. Since pharmaceutical, biotech, and health care firms are big employers, research skills are important, and candidates need to be good at multitasking.

Interview with a Professional:
Q&A
Stan Cieplinski

Accounting assistant/library technical services
Maricopa Community College District, Arizona

Q: *How did you get started?*

A: I got introduced to the job when I worked as a student assistant in the Serials/Government Documents Department of a university library. I was pursuing a B.A. degree at the time. My minor was in library science, so I thought that working in a library would be helpful.

Q: *What's a typical day like?*

A: I am mainly responsible for ordering books and media for our 11 libraries. My days are really busy. I have so many responsibilities, my supervisor even taught me time-management techniques so I could get everything done in an eight-hour day!

Hanging out with coworkers is definitely limited to before and after hours. Ordering takes up most of my workday. I organize order requests, choose vendors, check vendor inventories, create purchase orders, transmit the orders via EDI (Electronic Data Interchange) or fax, and cancel orders. I also manage vendor correspondence (paper and electronic). I work with our accounting department to set up vendors and verify budget numbers and amounts. Late in the day, I will process interlibrary loans. I am the contact person in our building who obtains materials for employee requests. I do the check-out and check-in work via our library system's circulation module. I package up all interlibrary loan (ILL) returns. I use programs like ILLiad ILL system and ICLC's First Search for ILL. At the end of the day, I am finally able to slow down long enough to check my phone messages and e-mail and respond to customer inquiries.

Q: *What's your advice for those starting a career?*

A: Be open-minded about the different types of work involved. Some tasks are really exciting, but others that are important to complete your required tasks can be tedious. You also need to accept change as a part of working in a library (changes in procedure, changes in technology, staffing changes in your area or with your customers and vendors).

Q: *What's the best part of being a library technician?*

A: Knowing that what you do is helping your customers in their quest for information. Even though I don't deal directly with library users, I do get the resources ordered and into their hands in a timely fashion.

Job Seeking Tips

Follow these suggestions and turn to Appendix A for help with résumés and interviewing.

- ✔ Get an associate's degree in this or a related field.
- ✔ Get volunteer experience and letters of recommendation.
- ✔ Join organizations in the field.
- ✔ Talk to the career placement office at your school.
- ✔ Check job hotlines and Web sites of institutions and organizations in the library field.
- ✔ Read books, magazines, and newspapers. Also, explore search engines on the Internet.
- ✔ Frequent bookstores and libraries.

Career Connections

For more information contact the following organizations:

American Library Association http://www.ala.org

Special Libraries Association http://www.sla.org

Council on Library/Media Technicians (COLT) http://colt.ucr.edu

LibrarySupportStaff.com http://www.librarysupportstaff.com

Associate's Degree Programs

Here are a few schools with well-regarded library programs:

Mesa Community College, Mesa, Arizona

Indian River Community College, Fort Pierce, Florida

College of Dupage, Glen Ellyn, Illinois

Long Island University, Post Campus, Brookville, New York

Financial Aid

Here is one source for library-related scholarships. Be sure to check with state and local library associations for opportunities in your area. Turn to Appendix B for more on financial aid for two-year students.

The **American Library Association** offers a number of scholarships for library support staff.   http://www.ala.org

Related Careers

Records clerk, medical records and health information technician, counter and rental clerk, statement clerk, and credit checker.

Fashion Designer

Vital Statistics

Salary: Fashion designers earn a median $55,000 a year, according to 2006 figures from the U.S. Bureau of Labor Statistics, but entry-level workers in this competitive field earn less than $30,000 annually.

Employment: The number of jobs for fashion designers is expected to remain at the present level of 17,000—a flat growth rate that places the occupation below the average for other jobs, according to figures from the Bureau of Labor Statistics. The best opportunities will be in design firms that design mass market clothing.

Education: A two-year degree in fashion design with courses in textiles, fabrics, ornamentation, apparel construction techniques, color and design theory, computer-aided fashion design, computer grading, marking and cutting, fashion sketching, history of costume, and pattern drafting is necessary.

Work Environment: Designers may work for clothing and textile companies, performing arts or broadcasting companies, museums, or retail stores. About 25 percent are self-employed, often working from their own studios. Designers usually create in very well-lit, airy spaces with room enough for bolts of fabrics, mannequins, sewing machines, and other tools of the trade.

What skirt length is in? What's the hot color this month? Fashion designers set the trends, and thanks to their ingenuity, consumers scour the stores hoping to find the latest look.

However, a career in fashion design is also a labor of love. The jet-setting lifestyle we often associate with fashion design is limited to a select few; for many, the work itself is the reward. For every Prada or Versace, there are thousands of designers who work long hours behind the scenes for manufacturers or struggle to win freelance contracts in a very competitive business. Also, styles change very quickly, and as the supermodel Heidi Klum says on the hit show *Project Runway*, in fashion "you're either in or you're out."

Fashion designers use flair and know-how to create everything from hospital uniforms to the eye-popping outfits worn by rock stars and models. To do this, they need a number of practical design skills. The work of the fashion designer is varied but usually includes the following:

- Sketching ideas and making patterns as guides to cutting product samples

- Selecting fabric and trimmings
- Visiting textile manufacturing and sales companies to keep current on the latest fabrics
- Dressmaking and tailoring, using patterns and draping to obtain the desired look for pants, shirts, jackets, dresses, and other clothes
- Fitting the finished garment
- Overseeing business affairs, including finances, marketing, and promotional activities, such as shows and displays
- Keeping up to date on fashion trends and competitors' merchandise and marketing

Although many designers initially sketch their designs by hand, many eventually digitize these sketches, using computer-aided design (CAD). This lets them view their designs on virtual models and in various colors and shapes, thus saving time by requiring fewer adjustments, prototypes, and samples later.

Most fashion designers create clothing, specializing in apparel for men, women, or children; others design footwear such as shoes and boots; and still others help produce accessories. Fashion designers who work for apparel wholesalers or manufacturers create designs for the mass market. These designs are manufactured in a variety of sizes and colors. On the flip side, a small number of designers create one-of-a-kind designs for individual clients, for which they usually charge very high prices. High-fashion designers may mix the making of original garments with designing clothes that follow established fashion trends, which they sell in their own retail stores or to upscale department stores. These designers may be self-employed or own small design firms.

Costume designers are fashion designers who specialize in creating for the performing arts, film, and television production. Their responsibilities are similar to those of other fashion designers. They perform extensive research into the styles worn at the time in which the story takes place and work with directors to find the right look for the characters. They make sketches of designs, select fabric and other materials, and oversee the production of the costumes. They also have to stay within the costume budget for the particular production.

On the Job

You may dream of seeing your creations on the runway, but if you decide to take the plunge into fashion design, get ready for the slap of reality. This is one demanding career. Working around the clock to finish original creations won't be enough. You'll also have to meet the highest standards of accuracy, taking exact measurements, and cutting patterns to precision.

Many steps are involved in designing clothing. Fashion designers have varying levels of involvement in this process depending on their experience and the size of the companies for which they work. Most designers begin by assisting more experienced designers. New designers usually are responsible for the technical work—the pattern making and sewing. In smaller firms, they may participate in the design process as well. As they gain experience, they assume greater levels of responsibility.

What most people don't realize about a creating a piece of clothing is how many people have to collaborate to do it. Since the people involved may be from different companies and in different areas, meeting deadlines can be difficult, which makes the work environment very stressful. Designers often divide their time among their own offices, clients' sites, and suppliers' locations.

Another element of stress comes from the fact that fashion seems to move at such a faster rate today than the past. Designers have very hectic schedules; there's often a lot of work to be done in a short period of time, especially if designers are rushing to meet a fashion show deadline. After an intensive stretch of work creating a line of clothing, the reward is often a runway show in which models parade before buyers, journalists, photographers, and others, showing off the new designs.

Freelance designers tend to work longer hours and in smaller, more congested spaces. Freelancers generally work on a contract basis and adjust their workdays to fit their clients' schedules and deadlines. They often meet with clients at night or on weekends. They also have to deal with the pressure of pleasing clients and finding new ones to maintain a steady income.

Most of the jobs in the field of fashion design in the United States are in New York and California. However, because of the global nature of the fashion industry, beginners also can get experience in one of the international fashion centers, such as Milan or Paris.

> **"I knew exactly what I wanted to do:**
> **I wanted to build a brand of clothing around**
> **my own attitude and my own lifestyle."**
> **—Tommy Hilfiger, a designer**

Keys to Success

To be a successful fashion designer, you need
- creativity
- patience with details
- art and design skills
- the ability to multitask

✏ organizational skills
✏ the ability to work well under pressure
✏ a good team-playing attitude
✏ awareness of trends
✏ complete dedication and ambition

Do You Have What It Takes?

If you spend endless hours poring through fashion magazines or putting together your own new looks, you may want to consider a career in fashion design. However, the glamorous allure of the fashion world draws a lot of competition, so you'll also need to have the talent and artistic vision to back up your ambition. To succeed you must be a fashion fanatic who is both creative and precise.

Beyond having artistic flair, you'll need real skills. Since many designers do rough designs by hand before creating digital files, you'll need the ability to sketch. Good teamwork and communication are critical as well, not only in developing designs, but also in selling them to buyers. Finally, designers should have a background in sewing and pattern making, both to make their own clothing and give proper instructions to others on how their designs should be constructed.

A Typical Day at Work

The world of fashion design is fast paced and the days are hectic, regardless of the size of the company. Experienced designers may be expected to research fashion trends, provide detail on what styles, colors, and fabrics will be popular for a particular season, choose fabrics to use with their designs, and then make prototypes of the garments. After they make last-minute adjustments, patterns are created and samples of the designs are made to show to store buyers. Depending on where you work you may be responsible for seeing fabric vendors, going to meetings, designing, following up on pattern making, completing paperwork, attending fittings, and designing graphics on the computer—all in the course of one day.

Designers who work for themselves have a little more control over their time: Some days they can choose to do more design; other days they can focus on getting ready to release the line or designing graphics, depending on the cycle of the season.

Many designers travel several times a year to trade and fashion shows to learn about the latest fashion trends. Designers also may travel frequently to meet with fabric and materials suppliers as well as the manufacturers who produce the final apparel products.

How to Break In

Many budding fashion designers develop their skills through internships with design or manufacturing firms. Others gain valuable experience working in retail stores, as personal stylists or custom tailors. This training gives them useful sales and marketing skills while they learn what styles and fabrics look good on a variety of people.

When starting out in their careers, future fashion designers take entry-level jobs as illustrators, pattern makers, stylists, or assistant designers. A career in merchandising is perfect for business-minded fashion design school graduates. As your career progresses, you may land a position as an associate or lead designer for an apparel company.

Two-Year Training

Most designers opt for some postsecondary education. However, many colleges and professional schools do not allow formal entry into their programs until a student has successfully completed basic art and design courses. When applying, you'll probably have to submit sketches and other examples of your creative ability. To prepare, immerse yourself in fashion through TV and magazines. Fashion is a cycle, and if you are aware of what is trendy now you may begin to see patterns in fashion history and understand how it works.

Once accepted, you'll study color, textiles, sewing, tailoring, pattern making, fashion history, CAD, and design of different types of clothing, such as menswear, swimwear, and formal dress. Coursework in human anatomy, mathematics, and psychology are also useful. Some fashion designers combine a fashion design degree with a business, marketing, or fashion merchandising education, especially those who want to run their own business or retail store.

What to Look For in a School

When considering a two-year school, be sure to ask these questions:

☞ Do the professors have experience in the fashion industry?

☞ Does student work look professional?

☞ Are there computers with the latest fashion design software?

☞ Will I have opportunities to show my work to industry experts?

☞ Is there a fashion club on campus?

☞ Are there exchange programs or tours of study in New York, London, Paris, and other centers of design?

☞ How are the internships and services for finding work after graduation?

☞ What is the school's overall reputation?

☞ Is the school located in or near a design center, such as New York City?

> **"Fashion design is a highly technical industry requiring great attention to detail and patience. It is this aspect that students often find most challenging."**
> —Mary Stephens, fashion design department chair, Fashion Institute of Design and Merchandising

The Future

The competition for jobs in this field is expected to remain high. Although people will always demand fresh new fashions, a continued decline in the U.S. manufacturing of clothes is seriously limiting job growth.

Opportunities in design firms that cater to high-end department stores and specialty boutiques may actually decline due to reduced demand for expensive, high-fashion items. However, jobs will be available in firms that design mass-market clothing sold in department stores and retail chain stores, since demand is increasing for stylish clothing among middle-income consumers.

Did You Know?

One of the most popular men's accessories, the necktie, started as a silk scarf that was worn by Croatian soldiers. Americans spend more than a $1 billion every year to buy a staggering 100 million ties.

Job Seeking Tips

Follow these tips on showcasing your creative ability and turn to Appendix A for help with résumés and interviewing.

✔ Build a good portfolio—a collection of examples of a person's best work. The portfolio is often the deciding factor in getting a job. You can start building a portfolio in high school and update it as you produce more work.

✔ Designers also can gain exposure to potential employers by entering their designs in student or amateur contests.

Interview with a Professional:
Q&A
Joseph S. Domingo
Joseph S. Domingo Studios, San Francisco, California

Q: *How did you get started?*

A: After I got my degree, I went to Los Angeles for a few years, where I worked for some manufacturing companies. While it was frustrating not to be working as a designer right away, I am really grateful for the production experience. I use it a lot now that I run my own design firm. Eventually, I moved back to San Francisco and worked as a freelance designer for a while. Eventually, I developed a following and was able to start my own business making custom-made sportswear, evening wear, wedding gowns, and contemporary clothing for men and women.

Q: *What's a typical day like?*

A: When I get to the studio, there are generally ongoing projects that I need to get back to. I might make a pattern for a design I've finished or research fabrics. Of course, there are always a lot of phone calls to return, and clients to talk to during the day as well.

Q: *What's your advice for those starting a career?*

A: Be sure to get as much training as possible. In addition to the courses you take in school, working as an intern or apprentice is invaluable. All designers have to pay their dues before they get recognized. It's important to be persistent too since there's a lot of competition out there. The bottom line? Stay humble and be willing to do whatever it takes.

Q: *What's the best part of being a fashion designer?*

A: I can't imagine doing anything else. The creativity, working with clients, there isn't anything about the work I don't like. While everybody has to earn enough to survive, it's also important to love what you do, and designing brings me a lot of joy.

Career Connections

For more information contact the following organizations:

International Association of Clothing Designers and Executives
http://www.iacde.org

Surface Design Association http://www.surfacedesign.org

American Association of Textile Chemists and Colorists
http://www.aatcc.org

Associate's Degree Programs

Here are a few schools with two-year fashion design programs:
Minneapolis Community and Technical College, Minneapolis, Minnesota
Houston Community College System, Houston, Texas
Harcum College, Bryn Mawr, Pennsylvania
Fashion Institute of Design and Merchandising, Los Angeles, California
Fashion Institute of Technology, New York, New York
Parsons School of Design, New York, New York
Academy of Art University, San Francisco, California

Financial Aid

Turn to Appendix B for information on financial aid for two-year students.

Related Careers

Buyer, fashion illustrator, retail clothes salesperson, and pattern maker.

Photographer

Vital Statistics

Salary: Photographers earn a median annual salary of about $26,000, according to 2006 data from the U.S. Bureau of Labor Statistics. Newspaper and periodical work pays more—$33,000 a year—than professional, technical, and scientific work, which pays $23,000 a year.

Employment: Job growth through 20014 should be as fast as the average for all occupations, although technological trends are both reducing barriers to entry in the field and allowing photography clients to work more with freelancers and part-time employees.

Education: A two-year degree should include basic courses in photography, including equipment, processes, and techniques. Some programs also offer business courses and training in design and composition.

Work Environment: Staff photographers work in settings that range from the newsroom to the portrait studio. Freelance photographers, such as those who work at weddings, often work out of their homes.

Photographs can sell products, report wars, or evoke happy

memories, but their effectiveness depends almost entirely on knowledge and artistic talent of the people behind the camera. Photographers use their artistic eye and technical know-how to capture the moment digitally or on film.

To create a successful picture you need to choose a subject, determine the effect you want, and select the appropriate equipment. In addition to a camera, photographers use a variety of other items—lenses, filters, tripods, flash attachments, and specially constructed lighting equipment—to improve the quality of their work.

Photography careers come in as many shapes and sizes as the images themselves. Commercial and industrial photographers take pictures of various subjects, such as buildings, models, merchandise, artifacts, and landscapes. Scientific, medical, and forensic photographers record images of a variety of subjects to illustrate or capture scientific and medical data or phenomena, using knowledge of scientific procedures. News photographers, also called photojournalists, photograph newsworthy people and places as well as sporting, political, and community events for newspapers, journals, magazines, or television. Fine arts photographers sell their photographs as artwork. Portrait photographers work with individuals and small groups (usually families). Some specialize in weddings, religious ceremonies, or school photographs and many work on location. Multimedia photographers create images used to illustrate Web pages and Internet sites.

Most salaried photographers work in portrait or commercial photography studios, while others work for newspapers, magazines, and advertising agencies. Photographers are needed in all areas of the country, but most find employment in metropolitan areas.

Self-employed, or freelance, photographers usually specialize in one of the mentioned fields. Some self-employed photographers have contracts with advertising agencies, magazine publishers, or other businesses to do individual projects for a set fee, while others operate portrait studios or provide photographs to stock photo agencies.

In addition to carrying out assignments under direct contract with clients, photographers license the use of their photographs through stock photo agencies or market their work directly to the public. Stock photo agencies sell magazines and other customers the right to use photographs, and pay the photographer a commission. These agencies require an application from the photographer and a sizable portfolio of pictures. Once accepted, photographers usually are required to submit a large number of new photographs each year.

Most photographers today store and edit their photos electronically. Many use digital cameras, allowing them to store and edit their work directly on computer, while some also use special silver halide film, which has to be developed and scanned before it can be edited on computer. Once the raw images have been transferred to the computer, they use processing software to crop or modify the images and enhance them through color correction and other specialized effects. Photojournalists and others interested in the accuracy of the provided image only use computers to produce their work and make no alterations to the image. Photographers who process their own digital images need to have computers, high-quality printers, and editing software, as well as the technical knowledge to use these tools effectively.

Because color film requires expensive equipment and exacting conditions for correct processing and printing, some photographers who use cameras with silver halide film send their film to laboratories for processing. Others develop and print their own photographs using their own fully equipped darkroom, especially if they use black-and-white film or seek to achieve special effects. Photographers who do their own film developing must invest in additional developing and printing equipment and acquire the technical skills to operate it.

On the Job

Just like their assignments, working conditions for photographers cover a wide range. Photojournalists work at crime scenes, fashion shows, and racetracks. Some operate in uncomfortable or even dangerous surroundings, especially news photographers, who cover accidents, natural disasters, civil unrest, or military conflicts. They must wait for hours in all kinds of weather for an event to take place and stand or walk for long periods while carrying heavy equipment. They also work under strict deadlines and frequently travel locally, stay overnight on assignments, and may even travel to distant places for long periods.

Photographers employed in government and advertising studios enjoy the luxury of working a five-day, 40-hour week. However, most other photographers work part time or on variable schedules. They often put in long, irregular hours and must be available on short notice. Portrait photographers usually take shots in their own studios, but they also travel for shoots on location, such as at a school, company office, or private home

In addition, these photographers spend only a small portion of their work schedule actually taking photographs. Their most common activities are editing images on a computer—if they use a digital camera—and looking for new business—if they are self-employed.

Self-employment allows for greater autonomy, freedom of expression, and flexible scheduling. However, income can be uncertain, and the continuous, time-consuming search for new clients can be stressful. Some self-employed photographers hire assistants who help seek out new business.

Keys to Success

Qualities that make for success in photography include

- imagination, creativity, and artistic ability
- patience
- computer savvy
- attention to detail
- knowledge of cameras, inside and out
- keen eye for lighting, backgrounds, and composition
- ability to work well with others

Do You Have What It Takes?

Since photography is as much a science as an art, a good photographer is equal parts technician and magician. If you're an artist with a techie side, you'll enjoy working with cameras and in the darkroom. In addition, you'll be able to master the computer software programs and applications that will allow you to prepare and edit images, and you'll be comfortable marketing directly to clients using the Internet to display your work. At the same time, however, you definitely need to be a visual thinker. Good photography demands artistic ability, good eyesight, and good hand–eye coordination.

Each specialization also requires its own skills and aptitudes. For instance, portrait photographers need the ability to help people relax in front of the camera. Commercial and fine arts photographers must be imaginative and original. News photographers must not only be good with a camera, but also understand the story behind an event so that their pictures match the story.

A Typical Day at Work

A photographer's "day" often starts the night before, when the equipment needed for the shoot gets packed. If you're shooting on location, whether it's a wedding or a horse race, everything has to be in place and in good working order. Therefore, the experienced photographer will probably check it all twice just to be sure.

Several kinds of action photography are relatively high-risk jobs. On an underwater shoot, for example, it's important to look out for yourself in water-filled—and possibly very narrow—passages. At the same time, you'll be carrying a large underwater camera system and trying to get the best possible photos. Some of the equipment you might take along are an Aquatica 5 camera with a Nikon F5 inside, a Nikonos V with a 15-mm lens, two Ikelite Substrobe 200 or 400 flashes, and lamps to illuminate the background or get the divers to light up another motif.

While not many photographers can expect to have such dramatic experiences, most workdays require them to:

- Select and test the equipment they plan to use
- Determine the composition of various shots and make technical adjustments to the equipment
- Use delicate instruments, such as optical microscopes attached to cameras
- Operate computers to manipulate photographic images
- Adapt existing photographic images and create new digitized images to be included in multimedia/new media products

Portrait photographers and others who own and operate their own businesses have other responsibilities in addition to taking pictures. They must arrange for advertising, schedule appointments, set and adjust equipment, purchase supplies, keep records, bill customers, pay bills, and—if they have employees—hire, train, and direct their workers. Many also process their own images, design albums, and mount and frame the finished photographs.

How to Break In

Those who succeed in landing a salaried job or attracting enough work to freelance are likely to be very creative, adept at operating a business, and able to master rapidly changing technologies.

One of the tricks to getting started is to "strut your stuff"—your creative and technical ability—with a dynamite portfolio. A collection of your best work will show how versatile you are at handling a range of subjects and locations. Some photographers enter the field by submitting an unsolicited portfolio of photographs to magazines and art directors at advertising agencies. For freelance photographers, a good portfolio is essential. They must present an individual style to differentiate themselves from the competition.

Employers usually seek applicants with a "good eye," imagination, and creativity, as well as a solid technical understanding of photography. Related work experience, on-the-job training, or some unique skill or talent (such as a background in computers or electronics) are also beneficial to prospective photographers.

Photographers may start out as assistants to seasoned photographers. Working with a pro, assistants learn a range of photography techniques and the skills needed to run a portrait or commercial photography business.

After several years of experience, magazine and news photographers may advance to photography editor positions. Some photographers teach at technical schools, film schools, or universities.

> # "You don't take a photograph, you make it."
> ## —Ansel Adams, photographer

Two-Year Training

Many community and junior colleges, vocational/technical institutes, and private trade and technical schools offer photography courses. Basic courses in photography cover equipment, processes, and techniques. Bachelor's degree programs, especially those including business courses, provide a well-rounded education. Art schools offer useful training in design and composition.

You may need special education or training for certain areas of photography. A medical photographer, for instance, who takes pictures of diseased skin (well, *somebody* has to do it!) will likely have to know about the medical background of the disease.

What to Look For in a School

When considering a two-year school, be sure to ask the following:

☞ Does the school offer a major in photography or art with a concentration in photography?

☞ Do you need to prepare a portfolio to be accepted into the school or the major?

☞ Does the program focus more on fine art or commercial photography?

☞ Does it emphasize darkroom photography over digital photography?

☞ Are the facilities well maintained and up to date? Do they have the latest computers and software as well as traditional equipment? Is the school's budget for technology strong?

☞ Are the teachers are knowledgeable of current advances in the field?

☞ What is the quality of the student work? What do they think of the school?

☞ Is there enough darkroom time and space available for students to do their work? How is darkroom time shared between majors and non-majors?

☞ How many courses outside the department will you take? Can you combine your photography degree with course work in business, teaching, or another related area?

☞ Are there any art museums or galleries on or near campus?

> **"If a day goes by without my doing something related to photography, it's as though I've neglected something essential to my existence, as though I had forgotten to wake up."**
> —Richard Avedon, photographer

The Future

This is a highly competitive field, especially for anyone interested in commercial and news photography. Job opportunities are being created by new Internet magazines, journals, and newspapers. The Internet is also making it easier for freelancers to market directly to their customers, increasing opportunities for self-employment.

However, as digital photography allows gifted amateurs to do the work of professionals, job growth may slow down. Also, the decline in the number of newspapers is affecting the demand for photographers. Salaried jobs in particular are becoming hard to find as more companies contract with freelancers rather than hire staff photographers.

Did You Know?

With a new photographic laser device developed to check damages on the space shuttle, NASA is going to help the FBI investigate crime scenes.

Interview with a Professional:
Q&A

Jerry Dodrill

Jerry Dodrill Photography, Bodega, California

Q: *How did you get started?*

A: I grew up with a camera in my hand and got serious when I started rock climbing. Photography was the best way to document my lifestyle, which evolved into a career. I have a gallery on California's north coast, do outdoor/adventure assignments, and license stock photos to publishers.

Q: *What's a typical day like?*

A: Look out the window from bed and decide whether to sleep in or go for a run on the beach and maybe take some pictures. Be at the office/gallery at 10 a.m., check and respond to correspondence, work on projects, and greet customers. Get the mail and hope there are more checks than bills.

Q: *What's your advice for those starting a career?*

A: Decide what you want in life and what makes you happy. There are those who chase the carrot, and those who run from the stick. Find a job that you believe in and would do even if you weren't getting paid. Are you happy living from job to job, or do you like the security of a regular check?

Q: *What's the best part of being a photographer?*

A: Being a photographer gives me the flexibility to chase my dreams, experience the most dramatic scenes/events our planet offers, and live an inspired lifestyle.

Job Seeking Tips

Follow the suggestions below and turn to Appendix A for help with résumés and interviewing.

✔ Get familiar with the field by subscribing to photographic newsletters and magazines.

✔ Join a camera club.

✔ Get summer or part-time work in camera stores, newspapers, or photo studios.

✔ Try to develop contacts.

✔ Gain technical and artistic skills.

✔ Build a good portfolio.
✔ Gain relevant experience (possibly through an internship).

Career Connections

For more information contact the following organizations:

Professional Photographers of America, Inc. http://www.ppa.com

National Press Photographers Association, Inc. http://www.nppa.org

American Society of Media Photographers, Inc. http://www.asmp.org

American Society of Picture Professionals
http://www.aspp.com/index.lasso

Professional Women Photographers Online
http://www.pwponline.org/

Visual Resource Association http://www.vraweb.org/resources.html

North American Nature Photography Association
http://www.nanpa.org/

"The photographer begins to feel big and bloated and so big he can't walk through one of these doors because he gets a good byline; he gets notices all over the world and so forth; but they're really unimportant—the important people are the people he photographs. They are what make him."
—Gordon Parks, photographer

Associate's Degree Programs

Here are a few schools offering quality associate's degree programs for photographers:

Paier College, Hamden, Connecticut

Corcoran College of Art and Design, Washington, DC

Art Institute of Pittsburgh, Pittsburgh, Pennsylvania

Pacific Union College, Angwin, California

Financial Aid

Here are a few sources for photography-related scholarships. Turn to Appendix B for more on financial aid for two-year students.

The National Press Photographers Foundation http://www.nppa.org

North American Nature Photography Association Foundation Grants http://www.nanpafoundation.org/grants.html

Milotte Scholarship Fund http://www.milotte.org

Related Careers

TV, movie, and video camera operator and editor; graphic designer and artist; art director; archivist; and Web designer.

Dance Instructor

Vital Statistics

Salary: Dancers who teach in schools or studios earn about $15 an hour, according to 2006 figures from the U.S. Bureau of Labor Statistics. That would make for yearly earnings of more than $30,000, except that salaried jobs in this field are few, and the majority of dancers earn less than $9 an hour, when they are able to work.

Employment: Employment for dancers will grow as fast as the average for all occupations through 2014—with dance enjoying a revival as recreation and exercise—but competition for those jobs will be intense. The 2002 Economic Census of the U.S. Census Bureau shows 6,504 dance studios, with receipts of about $1.3 billion, payroll of about $390 million, and about 38,000 employees—or a little more than $10,000 per employee in payroll.

Education: A two-year degree in dance, theater, or fine arts is required. Programs may emphasize modern dance but also offer courses in jazz, classical technique, dance composition, history, criticism, and movement analysis.

Work Environment: Generally, dancers and their teachers work in modern, climate-controlled facilities; however, some studios may be older and less comfortable.

When you see an incredible music, drama, or dance performance, the performers can make it seem easy and natural, but you're probably watching the culmination of years of training. Some major stars, such as Tom Hanks, credit their teachers with inspiring them, and some complete the cycle by becoming teachers themselves.

Because dance is strenuous and makes enormous physical demands on the body, many dancers stop performing by their late thirties. However, they often continue to work in the field as choreographers, dance teachers and coaches, or artistic directors. Younger dancers combine performing with teaching or choreographing. Many teachers find work in commercial dance studios and professional dance schools, while others find employment overseas.

Dance teachers may teach dance technique and artistic interpretation to other professionals or amateurs—both as individuals and in groups. Some focus on recreational dancing lessons such as ballroom dancing, while others prepare dance students for specific auditions and performances. In addition to helping perfect the dancer's performance, instructors often provide background in the cultural origins and symbolic meanings of classical, aboriginal, ethnic, or folkloric dances. Behind all the high steps, wiggles, and gyrations you see on a music video or Broadway play, there is an instructor who rehearsed the moves with the performers.

Teachers may specialize in one area of dance teaching or teach in a variety of areas. Full-time jobs for dance teachers are with dance companies, musical and theatrical productions, film and TV production companies, nightclubs, cruise ships, casinos, theme parks, and dance studios, as well as elementary and high schools and colleges and universities. Most major cities serve as homes to major dance companies; however, many smaller communities across the nation also support home-grown, full-time professional dance troupes.

On the Job

Many dance teachers are self-employed and work out of studios that are home based or rented. Others work in colleges or commercial studios. Still others work in nightclubs or on cruise ships.

In home studios and private dance schools, teachers are likely to have classes both during the day and at night. In high schools and colleges, they generally work regular school hours, but they also may have some evening commitments. Both types of teachers work weekends when taking classes themselves or putting on performances.

Teachers who coach musical productions and other family entertainment spend a lot of their time on the road. Similarly, if instructors work for a dance company, they may be on tour for part or most of the year; and the hours are long.

Dance is physically challenging, so dancers must exercise regularly and eat healthfully to stay trim and fit. It takes both passion and patience to pursue a career in this demanding field.

"Dancing is a sweat job."
—Fred Astaire, dancer

 Keys to Success

A successful dance instructor probably has

- ⚷ a strong aptitude and training in music and dance
- ⚷ good health and physical condition
- ⚷ an understanding of safety and injury prevention

- the motivation to teach children and adults of all abilities
- excellent communication skills
- patience and an interest in helping others to succeed
- ability to control groups and confidence to maintain order
- knowledge of how to run a business, if self-employed

Do You Have What It Takes?

If you have a love of dancing, like to be onstage, and enjoy teaching others what you know, dance education may be the career for you. At the same time, it's important to remember that pursuing a career in any aspect of dance also requires a willingness to eat smart, cross-train to prevent injuries, work nights and weekends, travel or tour frequently, and spend a lot of time in the studio and at rehearsal.

Above all, you'll need to be excited about teaching students with various skill levels and interests. Chances are few of them will be interested in pursuing professional performance careers, but the skills and qualities you'll bring out in them—including teamwork, discipline, and creativity—will be great preparation for whatever paths they choose.

A Typical Day at Work

A dancer's day is packed with activity. If you're teaching in a classroom—whether for a high school, college, or studio—your time will be organized by the administration. High school and college teachers generally work during the day, but teachers affiliated with studios may teach primarily at night.

What you teach will also be determined by the program with which you're affiliated. High school teachers, as well as many college instructors, are expected to teach the full spectrum—from ballet to ballroom, tap, and other forms of dancing. Studios tend to specialize more, so you will probably focus on only one or two types of dance as a studio teacher.

On any given day you may teach as many as five classes. If the course is just starting, you'll be expected to begin your classes by observing the students to determine their physical and artistic qualifications and limitations. After that, every class involves some time spent explaining and demonstrating techniques and methods for performing the movements associated with the dance steps you're teaching. You'll spend even more time drilling pupils in their execution of the steps.

Each session has its own dynamic. In some classes you may also want to include discussion on the history of dance. Or you may decide to add some material on the theory and practice of dance notation. If you're running your own studio, these variables all depend on your preferences and what types of dance your students may want to learn.

Your day will not necessarily end with your last class. Whether salaried or self-employed, many dance teachers supplement their teaching incomes with freelance work choreographing or directing dance performances; and dancers who run their own studios may finish off the work day by planning on ways to attract more students.

How to Break In

Some dancers enter the teaching arena immediately out of school; others wait until their careers as performers are finished or tapering down. However, professional performing experience does not automatically qualify someone to be a dance educator or assure a job. A Broadway dancer may not have any concept of what it's like to teach a seven-year-old or someone who isn't as gifted as he or she was as a child.

The completion of a college program in dance or drama and education is essential to qualify to teach dance in college, high school, or elementary school. Studio schools prefer teachers to have experience as performers.

Finding steady work in the fiercely competitive world of professional dance can be difficult. It takes both passion and patience to pursue a career in this demanding field. When you're ready to apply for a teaching job, be prepared to give some demonstration classes. Also, you may be expected to do choreography and present a video that displays your skill and versatility.

Two-Year Training

A good two-year program in dance education should offer courses in biomechanics and injury prevention, dance composition, dance history, performing arts design/production, performing arts directing, and teaching methods for dance.

Moreover, as a drama or dance education major, your schooling should comprise much more than lecture classes. Not only will you be performing in class and onstage, but you'll also be visiting schools to see performance education programs in action.

Before you graduate, the school should afford you an opportunity to spend a semester student teaching. Whether you're teaching tap dance to teens or playing theater games with third-graders, you'll learn how to manage a class, meet the needs of a variety of students, and keep classroom energy high but focused.

What to Look For in a School

When considering a two-year school, be sure to ask these questions:

☞ Is the program is accredited by the National Council for Accreditation of Teacher Education (http://www.ncate.org/) and your state board of education?

☞ Is the school accredited by the National Association of Schools of Dance (http://nasd.arts-accredit.org/) or the National Association of Schools of Theater (http://nast.arts-accredit.org/)?

☞ Does the program cover different approaches to performance and education?

☞ Will you be certified to teach after graduation?

☞ Is an audition required for admission?

☞ How many faculty members still perform?

☞ What well-known performers and educators regularly make visits to the school?

The Future

Historically, dancers and choreographers have faced intense competition for jobs. Only the most talented find regular employment. However, the growing popularity of dance for recreational and fitness purposes has resulted in an increase in teaching opportunities. The public interest in dancing may be behind the success of the ABC show *Dancing with the Stars*. As more people discover the joys of dance, national and regional dance companies may get a needed lift and offer more dance-related jobs. Opera companies and dance groups affiliated with colleges and universities and with television and motion pictures offer some opportunities as well. Finally, music video channels provide opportunities for both choreographers and coaches.

Job Seeking Tips

Follow these suggestions and then turn to Appendix A for help with résumés and interviewing.

✔ Research all the teaching opportunities in the area you want to live. Analyze which organizations are most compatible with your interests and training.

✔ Network with your school's alumni.

✔ If possible, prepare a video of yourself in performance that can be sent to and/or left with prospective employers.

✔ Be sure your résumé details all the different dance forms in which you are competent.

✔ List all the major roles you have danced on a separate attachment to your résumé.

✔ Tell everyone you know what you want to do.

✔ Get practical experience; try to intern or volunteer for a dance program.

✔ Get involved with organizations that promote dance education.

Interview with a Professional:
Q&A
Jacqui Young
Director, DanzJam/Push Factor dance company,
Long Island City, New York

Q: *How did you get started?*

A: I grew up as a dancer in a private dance studio. When I graduated from high school, I decided I might want to go to college for dance. So I enrolled at Northern Essex Community College. I never thought a community college would have a dance program but they did, and it was only 30 minutes from my home!

The Department of Dance chairperson convinced me to take as many dance classes as I wanted and just one academic class. She said, "If you hate it, you can drop out, but dancers need something to dance about, and choreographers need something to choreograph about. So if you are not educated, then what are you going to create from?"

I did not understand exactly what she was talking about at the time, but I took the one class; it was Western Civilization. Somehow I made it through that class and then took more classes—English composition, algebra, anthropology, etc.

Then I took dance composition. This class teaches you how to choreograph. We once danced with a chair for an entire class—about 45 minutes. After about 10 minutes, I was getting really frustrated. Then at some point I let go and began choreographing. This was so exciting that I wanted to do more. I could not wait to see what would be the next assignment. This was the beginning of my career as a teacher and a choreographer.

I was so excited about all this new information and all this new material that was pouring out of me that I began teaching all my new steps to the other dancers in the program. I have been teaching and choreographing ever since.

Q: *What's a typical day like?*

A: A typical day depends on the day. Wednesdays I wake at 7:30 a.m., do my morning things like brush my teeth, eat breakfast, feed the cats, etc. Then I work on the computer returning e-mails for about an hour. Then it is off to the rehearsal for my dance company, Push Factor.

I open the studio for rehearsal at 9:30 a.m. We have jazz technique class from 10 to 11:45 a.m., a 20-minute break, and then we work on choreography and repertory until 2 p.m. I close up the studio around 2:30 p.m., go to lunch with some of my dancers, and then we head to the office to make sales and marketing calls until 6 p.m. *(continued on next page)*

(continued from previous page)

I go back to the studio at 6:15 p.m. to teach a jazz class to high school students, and then I head home around 8:30 p.m. I am usually pretty tired by this point, and I order take-out and eat dinner while watching one of my favorite TV shows, *Lost*.

Q: *What's your advice for those starting a career?*

A: Getting the job you want is all about who you know as well as what you know. You need to get people to know about you. Once people know they can help you find the perfect place to work.

Some teachers get hired by studios where they are volunteering. Go to a studio and ask if you can be an assistant teacher and in return you get to take free dance classes at their studio. This will show the studio owner you are serious.

If you want to teach in the public school system, I recommend you get a degree in education of some kind. This will make it much easier, and if you have a degree in education, you can teach during the day and not just in the after-school programs. Take as many dance and teacher-training classes as you can.

Q: *What's the best part of being a dance teacher?*

A: The best part of being a dance teacher is I love my job. I get to wake up every morning and enjoy going to work. Also I get to wear comfortable clothes all day long. I do not need to buy expensive suits or high heels. I wear sweat pants and dance sneakers. I also love being creative and this is something I get to do on a daily basis. I create dances and costume the dances and light.

Did You Know?

The award-winning movie *Mad Hot Ballroom* is an inspiring look inside the lives of New York City schoolkids exploring the world of ballroom dancing.

Career Connections

For more information contact the following organizations:

Dance Educators of America http://www.deadance.com

Dance Masters of America http://www.dma-national.org

The National Dance Education Organization http://www.ndeo.org

Dance Teacher http://www.dance-teacher.com

National Association of Schools of Dance http://www.nasd.arts-accredit.org

Career Transitions for Dancers
http://www.careertransition.org/aboutmission.html

Answers4dancers http://www.answers4dancers.com

DanceMagazine http://www.dancemagazine.com

Dance/USA http://www.danceusa.org

The National Dance Association http://www.aahperd.org/nda/
template.cfm

Dancer.com http://www.dancer.com

Dance Art.com http:// www.danceart.com

Voice of Dance http://www.vcu.edu/artweb/dance/

Pointe Magazine http://pointemagazine.com

Dance/NYC http://www.dancenyc.org

TeachingArts.org http://www.TeachingArts.org

> **"I don't want people who want to dance, I want people who have to dance."**
> —George Balanchine, choreographer

Associate's Degree Programs

Here are a few schools with two-year dance programs:

Northern Essex Community College, Haverhill, Massachusetts

Dean College, Franklin, Massachusetts

Kilgore College, Kilgore, Texas

Scottsdale Community College, Scottsdale, Arizona

Foothills College, Los Altos, California

Financial Aid

Here are a few dance-related scholarships. Turn to Appendix B for information on financial aid for two-year students.

CTFD Educational Scholarships http://www.careertransition.org

The Caroline H. Newhouse Scholarship Fund
http://www.careertransition.org

Washington Post Music & Dance Scholarship Awards Program
http://www.washpost.com/community Look under
"The Post and Education."

Princess Grace Awards http://www.pgfusa.com

NFDI World Dance Scholarship
http://www.scn.org/nfdi/scholarship.html

Related Careers

Choreographer, artistic director, figure skater, gymnast, yoga or Pilates instructor, personal trainer, actor.

Musician

Vital Statistics

Salary: Pay for almost all musicians is hourly and averages about $18 per hour, according to 2006 figures from the U.S. Bureau of Labor Statistics. Higher earners are concentrated in the performing arts, and the lowest-paid work for religious organizations.

Employment: Growth in employment is projected to keep pace with the average for all occupations through 2014, but competition will be keen. Job creation will be strongest in religious organizations, according to the Bureau of Labor Statistics.

Education: A two-year degree in music, theater, or fine arts is necessary. In addition to skills training and practice, a two-year program often includes courses in music theory, interpretation, composition, or performance.

Work Environment: Musicians can (and often do) take their work anywhere. They may perform at private parties, in classrooms, or in theaters and concert halls to name a few locations

You love music and you want to share your passion with others. Your dream may be to become a hip-hop star in Los Angeles or a bluegrass fiddle player in Nashville, and hear an appreciative crowd clap and stomp its feet as you finish your electrifying set. No matter what sound strikes a chord with you, if you have a passion for performing, you might be destined for a career as a musician.

Musicians include a broad group of artists who play musical instruments, sing, compose, or arrange music in a variety of settings, solo or in groups. They may perform before live audiences or make recordings in music studios. Most musicians are known for a specific type of music—classical, country, ethnic, jazz, opera, or popular music—and they focus on a particular skill; for example, instrumental musicians play specific instruments such as the saxophone, trumpet, piano, guitar, drums, clarinet, or flute. The singer's instrument is his or her voice, which interprets the music. Composers create original music. Conductors lead orchestras and bands, and choral directors lead choirs and singing groups. Arrangers transcribe and adapt musical compositions to a particular style for orchestras, bands, choral groups, or individuals.

The music business is a tough field, but those in it usually feel impelled to perform their music, so much so that they're willing to make many sacrifices. Serious musicians spend a lot of time practicing and rehearsing, since it's a truism in the industry that "you're only as good as your last performance." Musicians also spend a significant amount of time on the road, traveling to and from performances.

Musicians devote a significant amount of time to looking for the next gig. The lucky few win a big contract with a recording studio or record label. Most, however, play and compose for many different kinds of employers. Musicians may get work scoring music or composing and arranging music for TV, movies, and commercials. The majority of musicians work in ensembles and perform live in nightclubs, concert halls, and theaters featuring opera, musical theater, or dance. Musicians often work at small-time gigs wherever they can—in clubs and churches, at weddings, birthdays, and bar mitzvahs—while waiting for that big break. With most performance work at night and on weekends, many musicians hold day jobs to round out their gainful activity.

Musicians face rejection all the time, but the most disciplined maintain confidence in their abilities; they can never allow themselves to become complacent if success is the goal. Because live audiences and auditions are a fact of life for musicians, they must be able to deal with their anxieties and deliver a quality performance in front of any audience.

Having more than one skill makes it easier to launch a career. Once employed, a musician's time is divided between performing (25 percent) and practicing (75 percent). This may either be alone or with their bands, orchestras, or other musical ensembles.

> **"Ability may get you to the top, but it takes character to keep you there."**
> **—Stevie Wonder, singer-songwriter**

On the Job

Musicians typically perform at night and on weekends. Full-time musicians with long-term employment contracts—including those who work for opera companies, orchestras, and TV and movie companies—enjoy steady work and a minimum of travel. However, club or recital musicians travel extensively to perform in a variety of local settings and may go on tour nationally or internationally.

Musicians spend most of their down time practicing or rehearsing. Most instrumental musicians work closely with a variety of other people, including their fellow musicians, agents, employers, sponsors, and audiences. Although they usually work indoors, some perform outdoors for parades, concerts, and festivals. In some nightclubs and restaurants, performers have to deal with cigarette smoke, poor lighting, and bad ventilation. The hours are likely to be irregular, including many nights and weekends. However, the thrill of performing and sharing your music with a live audience can be a great reward.

A career as a musician can be stressful, too. Whether recording or performing live, musicians may be under intense pressure to get it right. Plus, many live with the constant pressure to find work. This leads many musicians to accept permanent, full-time jobs in other fields, while they continue to freelance as musicians.

Keys to Success

To succeed as a musician you should have

- talent
- technical skill
- stage presence
- confidence
- self-discipline
- physical stamina

Do You Have What It Takes?

Whatever your goal, this career requires musical talent, versatility, creativity, poise, a good stage presence, and a strong competitive drive. Whether you're singing or playing an instrument, you also have to like being on stage.

Because musicians and singers always must make their performances look effortless, preparation and practice are important. Student musicians spend more time practicing than almost any other activity. Hours of practicing will help you learn to interpret a piece of music as the composer envisioned it. You'll also develop your own signature sound.

Valuable experience can be gained through playing in a school or community band or orchestra or with friends. Participate in as many performance groups as you can. Try everything from symphonic bands and chamber orchestras to choirs and a cappella groups. Music directors, composers, conductors, and arrangers need considerable related work experience or advanced training in these subjects.

As a performer, you'll need to be able to take constructive criticism from your colleagues and rejection when auditioning. Moreover, musicians who play in concerts or nightclubs and those who tour must have physical stamina to endure frequent travel and erratic schedules.

Learning a second language can help your career also. Opera singers are expected to know several languages.

A Typical Day at Work

Musician jobs vary widely but if you become member of a working band— as many novices in the field pay their dues—you'll be playing lots of shows, and that involves lots traveling, but it probably won't be first class.

On a typical day on the road, you may find yourself climbing out of a bunk on a bus that's headed for a college town in the middle of America. You and the rest of your bandmates start the day with a good hot breakfast at a diner.

You have to remind yourself what day and month it is—a tour can be disorienting. Since you have time before setting up for the show, you take a walking tour of the city you're playing. In the afternoon, you meet with the band to rehearse a brand new song and then you have to be at a local college radio station for an interview.

By later afternoon, you arrive at the club, where you help set up your gear, tune up, and perform a sound check to assure all your equipment is working correctly and you can all hear each other well on stage.

After a quick dinner, it's show time. All the lead-up has come down to one forty-five minute set. It goes without a hitch. Your take for the day— and it stops the minute you're off tour—is $125 after meals, plus the appreciation of the audience. After the gig, you socialize a little with the show promoter, club owner, and other musicians. Then you have to hurry and pile into your bus to start driving the long distance to your next show.

Two-Year Training

A good two-year program should include courses in music theory, music interpretation, composition, conducting, and performance in a particular instrument or voice. In preparation for professional careers, voice students learn, practice, and perform a variety of vocal pieces, from baroque arias to great nineteenth-century operatic roles. Opera singers-in-training also take classes in acting, movement, stagecraft, and even make-up.

You may have the chance to put your voice teacher's suggestions to the test while performing for your peers in a master class. In the most exciting master classes, big-name performers give feedback to students who perform in front of an audience—a sort of public private lesson.

How to Break In

Wondering how to get started in this field? Musical talent and ability, as demonstrated in an audition, are vital. In addition, the more versatile you are, the easier it is to find work. For example, instrumental musicians may play in a symphony orchestra or rock group, work in a studio band, or perform with an ensemble. Some play a variety of string, brass, woodwind, or percussion instruments or electronic synthesizers.

Your talent and reputation will help you get more gigs, and eventually you might want to get an agent to do your bookings and help you manage your career. Membership in a union related to your occupation or type of performance, such as the American Federation of Musicians, the American Guild of Musical Artists, or the American Federation of Television and Radio Artists, also may be required.

Many opera singers qualify for apprenticeship programs that opera companies sponsor for young singers who want to develop their repertoires. Some young musicians and singers pursue work in other countries, where there are more orchestras and opera companies than in the United States.

What to Look For in a School

When considering a two-year school, be sure to ask these questions:

☞ Does the school require an audition for admission?

☞ Where was the faculty trained?

☞ Do they still perform actively?

☞ How much private instruction is offered?

☞ How much space is there to practice and rehearse?

☞ How good are the acoustics?

☞ How many and what kinds of performance opportunities are there, both on and off campus?

☞ What is their quality?

☞ Is there a college radio or TV station?

☞ Does the college have a recording studio and offer opportunities for students to gain experience there?

☞ What opportunities are available on campus for students to help promote concerts and other arts events?

☞ What kinds of internships or summer programs are available?

☞ Is the program accredited by the National Association of Schools of Music?

The Future

Competition for work as a musician is intense; those who can play several instruments and perform a wide range of musical styles should enjoy the best job prospects.

Slower-than-average growth is expected for self-employed musicians, who generally perform in nightclubs, concert tours, and other venues, although many new salaried jobs for musicians are projected in religious organizations. Also, new outlets have developed for musicians over the past few decades, including cable television, sophisticated video and computer games, and satellite radio.

Interview with a Professional:
Q&A

Joshua Rasmussen
Band teacher, Sevier School Distric, Richfield, Utah

Q: How did you get started?

A: I really enjoyed music in high school. I sang in the concert choir and played trumpet in the concert and jazz bands. When I entered college, I had not decided on a career. I wanted to become a better musician, so I decided to major in music. My emphasis was music education, although I wasn't sure that I wanted to be a music teacher. I had some great mentors who encouraged me and helped me stay the course. Before I finished student teaching, two schools contacted me requesting an interview. I accepted my current job before I graduated.

Q: What's a typical day like?

A: My day is split between two schools. The high school program has 90 students, and the middle school program has 150. I start my day at 6:30 a.m. I direct a jazz ensemble and I also teach a percussion class at the high school. In the afternoon I teach at the middle school, where classes are assigned according to age. The sixth-graders take Beginning Band; the seventh-graders, Intermediate Band; and the eighth, Advanced. Every band presents several concerts, and participates in at least one music festival annually. The high school bands consistently receive top honors at regional and state festivals. They also march in parades, play at home sporting events, and are often invited to perform for community events. I direct a middle school jazz band two days a week after school. I spend the other days working with small groups or individuals at both schools. I usually head home around 4:30 or 5, but during the football and basketball seasons return to the high school at 6 for the games.

Q: What's your advice for those starting a career?

A: Great interpersonal skills are the most valuable assets of successful people in any profession. There are many great musicians in the world, but in order to be a successful teacher, you have to know how to talk with people. It is also very important to become proficient on your primary and secondary instruments. I also recommend learning to play the piano. Playing piano makes you a better musician because you learn to understand relationships between melody and harmony. Unlike many other instruments, piano is very visual. You not only hear, but also you can see exactly what is going on in the music. I'd also advise exploring all different kinds of music,

(continued on next page)

(continued from previous page)

attending live performances, and getting to know musicians and educators. Finally, I believe the best way to learn something is by teaching it to someone else. Take every opportunity to help less experienced musicians.

Q: *What's the best part of being a musician?*

A: Of course I love performing; but the best part of my job is the group of kids I teach. I can't say enough about my students. They are smart, involved, dependable, and willing to work hard. I really enjoy seeing them succeed.

Did You Know?

Some of today's top pop stars are getting their start on TV talent shows such as *American Idol*. Kelly Clarkson, a former waitress from Texas, beat out nine other finalists in this televised competition and won a recording contract with RCA Records. Her album, *Breakaway*, went triple platinum.

Job Seeking Tips

Follow these suggestions and turn to Appendix A for help with résumés and interviewing.

✔ Know the market/industry.

✔ Network.

✔ Find your niche.

✔ Maintain a professional attitude.

✔ Think like an entrepreneur.

Career Connections

For more information contact the following organizations:

National Association of Schools of Music
http://www.nasm.arts-accredit.org

American Federation of Musicians
http://www.afm.org/public/home/index.php

American Guild of Musical Artists http://www.musicalartists.org/

Music Industry Career Center http://www.music-careers.com

Associate's Degree Programs

Here are a few schools with well-regarded music programs:

Bucks County College, Newtown, Pennsylvania

Casper College, Casper, Wyoming
Joliet Junior College, Joliet, Illinois
Montgomery College, Rockville, Maryland
Hillsborough Community College, Tampa, Florida

> **"Don't worry about what others say about your music. Pursue whatever you are hearing . . . but if everybody really hates your music maybe you could try some different approaches."**
> —Wynton Marsalis, musician

Financial Aid

Here are some music scholarships. Turn to Appendix B for more on financial aid for two-year students.

Glenn Miller Birthplace Society http://www.glennmiller.org

National Foundation for Advancement in the Arts http://www.artsawards.org

Young Musicians Foundation Scholarship Program http://www.ymf.org

AMCA Scholarship Fund http://amcofa.org

Talbots Women Scholarship Fund http://www.talbots.com

Jack Kent Cooke Young Artist Award http://www.jackkentcookefoundation.org

School Band and Orchestra Magazine Scholarship http://www.sbomagazine.com

Davidson Fellows http://www.davidsonfellows.org

Related Careers

Teacher, songwriter, music therapist, instrument repairer and tuner, music librarian, critic, disc jockey, concert manager, booking agent, and publicist.

Broadcast Engineering Technician

Vital Statistics

Salary: Broadcast engineering technicians earn a median annual income of about $28,000, according to 2006 data from the U.S. Bureau of Labor Statistics. Television stations in large markets pay best; small marktcts and radio stations tend to pay less.

Employment: Jobs for broadcast engineers are project to grow at the same rate as for all other jobs through 2014, according to the Bureau of Labor Statistics. Competition for work will be less keen in small towns than major cities.

Education: A two-year degree in broadcast technology, or electronic or computer networking.

Work Environment: Broadcast engineers may work indoors in broadcasting maintenance centers, radio and television studios, or outdoors at transmitting stations. When doing maintenance work, they may climb poles or antenna towers, or do heavy lifting while setting up equipment.

Have you ever watched a newscast and had a picture come on that didn't match the story? The person at the TV station who is responsible for making sure this doesn't happen is the broadcast engineer.

Broadcast engineers work mainly at radio and television broadcasting networks and stations. When other broadcasting staff can't solve a problem (or don't want to handle a problem), they usually contact the engineer. Engineers are facilitators who make things work. They install, test, repair, set up, and operate the electronic equipment used to record and transmit radio and television programs, cable programs, motion pictures, and streaming video for the Internet. Another interesting aspect to being a broadcast engineer is that over the past few years, they have become computer and network administrators. The terms *operator*, *engineer*, and *technician* are often used interchangeably to describe their jobs.

With such a range of work, many technicians specialize. Some produce movie soundtracks in film production studios; others control the sound of live events such as concerts, or record music in a recording studio. Because television news coverage requires so much electronic equipment and the technology is changing so rapidly, many stations assign technicians exclusively to news. Chief engineers, transmission engineers, and broadcast field supervisors oversee technicians and maintain broadcasting equipment.

About 30 percent of broadcast engineers work in broadcasting, mainly for radio and television stations, and 17 percent work in the motion picture, video, and sound recording industries. Television stations employ, on average, many more technicians than do radio stations. Some technicians are employed in other industries, producing employee communications, sales, and training programs.

Technician jobs in television and radio are located in virtually all cities; jobs in radio also are found in many small towns. The highest paying and most specialized jobs are concentrated in New York City, Los Angeles, Chicago, Atlanta, and Washington, D.C. Motion picture production jobs are concentrated in Los Angeles and New York City.

The transition to digital recording, editing, and broadcasting has greatly changed the work of broadcast and sound engineering technicians and radio operators. Software on desktop computers has replaced specialized electronic equipment in many recording and editing functions. Most radio and television stations have replaced videotapes and audiotapes with computer hard drives and other computer data storage systems. Computer networks linked to specialized equipment dominate modern broadcasting.

On the Job

At large stations and networks, technicians usually work a 40-hour week, although they may be under great pressure to meet broadcast deadlines and may occasionally work overtime. Technicians at small stations routinely work more than 40 hours a week. Evening, weekend, and holiday work is usual because most stations are on the air 18 to 24 hours a day, 7 days a week. Even though a technician may not be on duty when the station is broadcasting, some technicians may be on call to handle emergencies.

As a rule, broadcast engineering technicians work indoors in comfortable surroundings. If they are responsible for broadcasting news and other programs from locations outside the studio, however, they may work outdoors and in all types of weather. Technicians who do maintenance may also have to do physical work—running cables, climbing transmitting towers, and carrying heavy equipment.

Keys to Success

To succeed in broadcast engineering, it is helpful to possess

- manual dexterity
- an aptitude for working with electrical, electronic, and mechanical systems and equipment
- a sharp eye and a keen ear
- high energy

Do You Have What It Takes?

Are you an electronics geek who likes to set up, operate, and work on the "bugs" in equipment? Are you a stickler for perfection? These qualities are essential for a career in broadcast engineering.

In addition to the interest and ability to work with mechanical, electrical, and electronic systems, prospective technicians need good manual dexterity. You should be the type of person who has built electronic equipment from hobby kits or operated an amateur, radio. For both radio and TV, knowledge of software is mandatory. Many in the field come by valuable experience and technical know-how through volunteering with college and university radio and television stations.

A Typical Day at Work

Technician jobs vary a lot from day to day and job to job. In large stations and at the networks, the work is fairly specialized, but a technician in a small studio may be more of a jack of all trades, performing many different duties in the course of a day.

If your assignment is in the control room of a radio or television broadcasting studio, you may spend your day operating the control panels that select the source of the material being broadcast. You may switch the broadcast from one camera or studio to another, from film to live programming, or from network to local programming. Through the use of hand signals and headsets, you'll give technical directions to your coworkers in the studio. You will also be involved in operating equipment that regulates the signal strength, clarity, and range of sounds and colors of recordings or broadcasts.

In a small studio, you might also work hands-on television cameras, microphones, tape recorders, lighting, sound effects, transmitters, antennas, sound consoles, and other gear. You may monitor and log outgoing signals, operate transmitters, and set up, adjust, service, and repair electronic broadcasting equipment.

How to Break In

Beginners often start their careers in small stations and, once they get some experience, move on to larger ones. Job applicants face stiff competition in major metropolitan areas, where pay is higher generally, so opportunities are greater in small cities and towns.

When starting out, broadcast engineers acquire skills on the job from more senior technicians and supervisors. Working in a studio as an assistant is a great way to gain experience and knowledge.

Large stations usually hire only technicians with experience. Technicians who have mastered the job can become supervisory technicians. Many employers pay tuition and expenses for courses or seminars to help technicians keep abreast of developments in the field. A college degree in engineering is needed in order to become chief engineer at a large television station.

In the movie industry, people are hired as apprentice assistants and work their way up to more skilled jobs. Employers often hire experienced freelance technicians on a picture-by-picture basis. Reputation and determination are important in getting jobs.

Licensing is not required for broadcast engineers. However, certification by the Society of Broadcast Engineers is a mark of competence and experience. The certificate is issued to experienced technicians who pass an exam.

Two-Year Training

Technical school, community college, or college training in broadcast technology, electronics, or computer networking provides a solid educational background for entering this career. In a broadcast technology program, you'll study everything from electronics and digital audio formats to government regulations and math. Two-year students often can get crucial hands-on training by interning or volunteering at a school radio or television station.

What to Look For in a School

When considering a two-year school, be sure to ask these questions:

☞ Is there equipment for television production as well as film?

☞ Are the studios and labs comfortable and well equipped?

☞ Are computers up to date with current software?

☞ Will the college help you find work after graduation?

☞ What jobs do recent grads have now?

Did You Know?

Even with all the attention that has been paid to the Internet, Americans still get the vast majority of their news and information from TV and radio broadcasts.

Interview with a Professional:
Q&A
Jim Marco
Director of engineering, WSTM/WSTQ,
Syracuse, New York

Q: *How did you get started?*

A: I was always fascinated with radio in general but knew I wanted to do electronics. My older brother was a disc jockey at the local hometown radio station, and I used to go and watch him work along with the station's chief engineer. I made a general pest of myself, asking a lot of questions of the chief engineer and begging the station manager for a job. My persistence paid off, and I got a job there. It was as a news announcer, not an engineer, but it got me in the door. From there, I moved into the control room and eventually into engineering over a three-year period. I was especially interested in the tower and transmitter facility and developed some expertise in that arena. I sort of fell into television by accident. The station I started at needed someone with the appropriate FCC license to operate their remote transmitter facility. I learned a lot about the operation and equipment on the job and then progressed into engineering management.

Q: *What's a typical day like?*

A: There really is no typical day, which is one of the really neat things about broadcast engineering. Sure, there are routine tasks that need to be performed each day, but there are unexpected challenges and opportunities as well. Broadcast engineers are facilitators. We create the technical environment that allows everyone else in the operation to accomplish their goals. Many times we have to create solutions on short deadlines with no money or other resources. It can be a headache and a rush, but it certainly is not boring.

Q: *What's your advice for those starting a career?*

A: You have to be willing to do any job, work any hours, and bring a solid work ethic and passion to everything you do. I have been fortunate to teach as an adjunct instructor for more than 20 years. I spend a lot of time talking about passion and work ethic. Unfortunately, many students I interview for jobs have unrealistic expectations about what to expect when entering the broadcast field. They carry a sense of entitlement that does not fit in any modern work environment. It sets them up for disappointment and failure before they even get started. That needs to change at the most fundamental levels.

(continued on next page)

(continued from previuos page)

Q: *What's the best part of being a broadcast engineering technician?*

A: Variety. I never know from one day to the next what challenges are waiting for me. Also, I get to work with each and every person in the organization on a daily basis. I personally like that. It gives me a fresh perspective on how things work together and the direction that the industry is moving.

The Future

In the next decade, the overall employment of broadcast engineering technicians is expected to grow about as fast as average for all occupations, according to the U.S. Bureau of Labor Statistics. Job growth in radio and television broadcasting will be limited by consolidation of ownership of radio and television stations and by labor-saving technical advances, such as computer-controlled programming and remotely controlled transmitters.

Employment of broadcast engineers in cable and pay television should grow faster than the average as the range of products and services expands. Employment of these workers in the motion picture industry is also expected to grow rapidly. However, job prospects will remain competitive because of the large number of people who are attracted by the glamour of working in motion pictures.

"Engineering is the conscious application of science to the problems of economic production."
—H. P. Gillette, engineer

Job Seeking Tips

Follow these suggestions and turn to Appendix A for help with résumés and interviewing.

- ✔ If you are in college, get involved with your school radio or TV station.
- ✔ Look into internships and training programs; many stations offer them.
- ✔ Check with your college's career center.
- ✔ On breaks and vacations, seek out volunteer opportunities with your local radio station.
- ✔ Be prepared to start as production assistant or camera operator.

Career Connections

For more information contact the following organizations:

Society of Broadcast Engineers http://www.sbe.org

National Association of Broadcasters http://www.nab.org

International Cinematographer's Guild
http://www.cameraguild.com/

National Association of Broadcast Employees and Technicians
http://www.nabetcwa.org

> **"What you want is someone with a natural inclination for the technical side. Ideally speaking, you want to hire a person with a tech history as well as some formal in-class training."**
> —**Kevin McNamara, veteran station chief engineer**

Associate's Degree Programs

Here are a few schools with well-regarded broadcast engineering programs:

Cuyahoga Community College, Cleveland, Ohio

Cayuga Community College, Auburn, New York

Central Carolina Community College, Sanford, North Carolina

St. Louis Community College, St. Louis, Missouri

College of DuPage, DuPage, Illinois

Modesto Junior College, Modesto, California

Financial Aid

Here are some sources for scholarships related to broadcast engineering. Turn to Appendix B for more on financial aid for two-year students.

BEA National Scholarships in Broadcasting
http://www.beaweb.org

The John Bayliss Broadcast Foundation
http://www.baylissfoundation.org

The Freedom Forum http://www.freedomforum.org

La Raza Media Educational Fund Phone: 510-261-1677

Asian American Journalists Association http://www.aaja.org

American Women in Radio and Television http://www.awrt.org

Related Careers

Camera operator and editor, composer, computer support specialist, electrician, electronics technician, engineering technician, and program director.

Interior Designer

Salary: The median annual income for interior designers is about $40,000, according to 2006 figures from the U.S. Bureau of Labor Statistics, but many compete to make those dollars, and the lowest earners make less than $20,000.

Employment: Employment in this field is projected to grow as fast as the average for all careers through 2014. One third of interior designers are self-employed.

Education: A major in interior design, architecture, or a related field, such as engineering, is a good starting point for this career.

Work Environment: Designers may work in their own office or their client's home or office.

Interior design is a widely misunderstood profession. Some people have the notion this business is only about choosing colors, working with beautiful fabrics, and being creative all day long day, but that's not the case.

Interior design involves integrating the skills of an artist with those of an engineer and businessperson. *Interior designers* plan the space and furnish the interiors of private homes, public buildings, and commercial establishments. They may also plan additions and renovations. *Interior decorators,* on the other hand, are concerned with finishing elements of a home or office building.

Designers work closely with architects and clients to determine a style that best suits the structure of the space and the needs of the client while working within the confines of a specified budget. They need to know about electrical capacity, safety, and blueprints, and they often visit the job site while it is under construction to better plan their designs.

Designers make drafts or drawings by hand or with a computer. Most use computer-aided design (CAD) tools. Designers need up-to-date computer and telephone equipment.

Professionals have to be familiar with the nature of wood, color, textiles, fabric, and decorating products such as paint and wallpaper. They should be knowledgeable about the historical periods that have influenced the development of furniture style and room design as well.

Interior designers also must master budgeting and communications. Presentations for client approval usually include a sketch or scaled floor plan showing furniture arrangement, color charts, and samples of upholstery, draperies, and wall coverings. The complete proposal includes an estimate of the cost for the installation.

After the proposal is accepted, interior designers assemble furnishings and act as agents for their clients by contracting and supervising the services of craft workers. They shop in wholesale markets to locate furnishings and accessories, and, when necessary, design original pieces to be made to order. They must be able to negotiate with installers, pay furniture manufacturers, keep accurate billing records, ensure the codes for local municipalities are met, acquire all the materials for the job, and schedule the laborers who will complete the design elements.

Businesses that employ interior designers include interior and finishing construction firms, architectural, engineering, and other scientific companies, business service firms, and general merchandise stores. Interior designers in many states must earn a license, register with the state, and pass the National Council for Interior Design exam in order to practice. Even for those states that do not require the exam, membership in a professional organization can enhance one's reputation. To be eligible, a designer must have at least six years of combined experience and education, with at least two years at a design school.

> ## "Decorate your home. It gives the illusion that your life is more interesting than it really is."
> —Charles M. Schulz, cartoonist

On the Job

Most designers work in offices, but they also spend a lot of the time traveling, meeting with clients, consulting with contractors on construction sites, and shopping for design elements.

Designers frequently work overtime, but most have flexible work hours. They generally work anywhere from 40 to 70 hours a week. They usually set schedules to please their clients, making sure to meet deadlines and stay on budget.

Those who are paid by contract are under stress to please clients and find new ones to keep a steady income. They often face masses of paperwork, ranging from purchase orders to estimates.

Keys to Success

For success as an interior designer, it helps to have

☙ an eye for color and detail

☙ creativity

❧ problem-solving abilities
❧ communications skills
❧ computer knowledge

Do You Have What It Takes?

Do you have a passion for the visual and fine arts? Are you good at arranging the furniture, posters, and other items in your room? Interior design is a career for people who are creative, imaginative and artistic. Good interior designers are able to create indoor spaces that not only look good but also function well. Their designs have to suit the intended purpose of the building—whether it's an office, hospital, classroom, or spa. Each of these has its own purpose—from raising workers' productivity to helping people relax—and the design requirements are different for each.

Interior design and decorating is also a people business. You must be comfortable meeting and dealing with clients, tradespeople, craftsmen, builders, and more. You have to communicate clearly and effectively, as well as listen attentively. Because you often work in collaboration with architects, contractors, and other service providers, you need to be both a good team leader and a good team player. You must be willing to negotiate and mediate when necessary to solve problems.

As an interior designer, you also must know how to balance practical with aesthetic considerations. Although a client's style may not match your own, you have to please the person writing the checks, and you also have to work within the restrictions of building codes. If you know your way around a computer, you have a head start into this career. To impress clients and explain your vision, you will need to generate three-dimensional presentations, animated walkthroughs, and scaled dimensional space plans—all using computer design.

How to Break In

Most interior designers begin their careers through internships, studying and learning on the job. The National Council for Interior Design Qualification (NCIDQ) offers the Interior Design Experience Program to help entry-level designers get work experience. However, part-time or summer employment in the furniture department of a retail store or with a large architectural firm also can provide good basic training and may lead to a permanent job.

Whenever you can, find opportunities to design and decorate spaces, like theater sets or special-event locations. Keep photos of your work in a portfolio. Don't forget: Even to be accepted as an intern, it is necessary to show your creative ability and present a record of your related experience and studies.

Through every stage, from novice to expert, this career requires continuous learning. New interior, graphic, and industrial and commercial designers get on-the-job training. For community college grads, it will be necessary to stay in an apprentice position for four years in order to quality for the NCIDQ test you'll need to get licensed.

A Typical Day at Work

Designers' workdays can be pretty fast-paced and hectic, partly because they are usually juggling multiple projects. Your day might begin with a client meeting to discuss plans for an addition to the client's home. Over bagels and coffee, you discuss how to best use the two new rooms, how much they want to spend, and when they need the project completed.

Your meeting may be followed by a trip to the local flea market to hunt for a Victorian lamp for another client or a visit to the design center to research the costs and availability of contemporary desks for a home office. While there, you invest in a book of fabric swatches you've been meaning to pick up.

Back at the office, there's a ton of e-mail to sort through: cost estimates from a couple of plumbing contractors on a new bathroom; a note from a client who's decided that the blue you agreed on for the exterior of their new home is too dark (even though it was just painted); and the architect's plans for the interior of some condos on which you'll be working.

After filing the plumbing estimates with the other information on the new bathroom, you decide to call the new homeowner to see if you can convince them that the blue blends perfectly with their neighbors' homes and is very authentic for the colonial style of the house. You've already done your research on the Asian furnishings this builder has stipulated, and now that you've got the architectural specifications, you can start drawing floor plans and designing a couple of model rooms. After studying the material for a half hour or so, you turn on your computer, bring up CAD, and start inputting the basic specs.

You get to spend about a half hour on this before you're interrupted by one of several phone calls: the homeowner wants to know the date the painter is scheduled; and so it goes. By the end of the day, you've got most of your data input, found out from the electrician where the outlets will go in the condos, and—oh yes—put a call in to the painter to fix the blue!

Two-Year Training

Whether you major in design, architecture, or engineering, you'll need to take courses in history of design, interior design finish materials, interior design theory, graphic communications, and professional practice. Two-year training can provide you with a strong foundation to start along this career path. Those dedicated to interior design may continue with their education after earning an associate's degree.

What to Look For in a School

When considering a two-year school, be sure to ask these questions:

☞ Does the department concentrate more on architecture and construction, or visual effects and personal expression?

☞ How many professors are in the department?

☞ Do students take on a variety of challenging projects?

☞ Do studios and computer labs have the latest equipment?

☞ Do students have their own work spaces?

☞ Is the department accredited by the Foundation for Interior Design Education Research?

The Future

Employment of most types of designers is expected to grow as fast as the average for all occupations through the year 2014. As homeowners and businesses spend more on design, additional interior design jobs will be created. Demand for interior design services in the hospitality industry—hotels, resorts, and restaurants—is expected to rise due to increases in tourism. Many new retirement communities and nursing homes also will be built to accommodate an aging population.

Prospective designers can expect to face keen competition for jobs, because many talented people want to get into this creative and potentially lucrative field.

Job Seeking Tips

Follow the suggestions below and turn to Appendix A for advice on résumés and interviewing.

✔ Practice at home.

✔ Build a portfolio of samples of your creative work.

✔ Make contacts in the field.

✔ Volunteer your services.

✔ Establish relationships with suppliers.

✔ Keep up to date on new construction in your community and contact the firms that have been retained to work on it.

✔ Continue to study different styles.

Interview with a Professional:
Q&A
Bete Gerula

District representative, Koroseal Wall Covering,
Virginia Beach, Virginia

Q: *How did you get started?*

A: I got into this field because the manager of my building asked if I was available to help paint balconies. This led to installing wall coverings, and after I got several design clients, I decided to go back to school. Since I got my degree, I have run my own interior design business. I started by restoring small offices and eventually managed large hotel renovations.

Q: *What's a typical day like?*

A: When I first started, 50 to 60 percent of the time was spent doing the actual work. I also had to spend a portion of each day returning calls and meeting with clients. At some of these meetings, I would make presentations; at others I would help them make selections.

Q: *What's your advice for those starting a career?*

A: It's important to do your homework. There's more to designing than just creativity. It's a process of gathering information. You need to be sure you're as clear as possible on what the customer wants. So you need to work on your presentation and people skills.

Q: *What's the best part of being an interior designer?*

A: I really like the client contact. Also seeing the transformation and getting a good end result.

Did You Know?

According to people in the know, combining yellow and black produces the most visually conspicuous color combination.

Career Connections

For more information contact the following organizations:

American Society of Interior Designers http://www.asid.org/

Dezignare Interior Design Collective http://www.dezignare.com/

International Furnishings and Design Association
http://www.ifdaef.org

International Interior Design Association http://www.iida.org/

Interior Design Associations Foundation http://www.idaf.us/

Council for Interior Design Accreditation http://www.accredit-id.org/

Associate's Degree Programs

Here are a few schools with well-regarded interior design programs:

Bellevue Community College, Bellevue, Washington

Lansing Community College, Lansing, Michigan

Pellissippi State College, Knoxville, Tennessee

Financial Aid

Here are some interior design scholarships. Turn to Appendix B for more on financial aid for two-year students.

International Furnishings and Design Association Student Scholarship http://www.ifda.com

Worldstudio Foundation Scholarship http://worldstudio.org

American Society of Interior Designers Educational Foundation Scholarships http://www.asid.org

Related Careers

Architect, graphic designer and illustrator, industrial designer, retail salesperson, set designer, and window dresser.

Audio Technician

Vital Statistics

Salary: Audio technicians earn a median annual salary of $32,570, according to 2006 data from the U.S. Bureau of Labor Statistics.

Employment: Job growth for audio technicians is projected to grow faster than the average for all occupations through 2014, according to 2006 data from the Bureau of Labor Statistics.

Education: Technical school, community college, or college training in broadcast technology, electronics, or computer networking provide the best preparation.

Work Environment: Most audio technicians work in clean, well-lighted studios, but audio recording techs can work outside, too, at concerts and other events.

Picture yourself controlling a huge soundboard in a control booth. You're helping create a best-selling CD for the hottest band in town. Afterward the wrap party rocks. Such is the life of an audio recording technician. Maybe it's not the whole life, but it's certainly a small but rewarding part of this career.

Audio recording, also known as sound engineering, is all about capturing sound. It involves both production and post-production tasks. The production part may be everything from set-up to the actual recording. Post-production (after recording) is when the raw recorded material gets polished or morphed into what you want it to sound or look like. That can involve editing and changing the recorded sounds by altering the pitch, adding reverb, and other audio techniques.

As an audio technician, you may operate machines and equipment to record, synchronize, mix, or reproduce music, voices, or sound effects. You may be involved in the production of radio or television broadcasts, concerts, plays, musical recordings, television shows, and movies. You may work in a variety of settings as well—recording studios, radio stations, sporting arenas, theaters, and movie and TV studios.

The terms *operator, engineer,* and *technician* often are used interchangeably to describe these jobs. In large organizations, audio technicians often have specialized responsibilities. Some run equipment designed to produce special audio effects, such as the sounds of thunder or a police siren. Sound mixers or re-recording mixers produce soundtracks for movies or television programs. After filming or recording is complete, these specialists insert sounds and voices through a process called *dubbing.* Field technicians focus on setting up and operating portable transmission equipment at locations outside the studio.

The transition to digital recording has greatly changed the work of broadcast and sound engineering technicians and radio operators. Software on desktop computers has replaced specialized electronic equipment for many recording and editing functions. Most radio and television stations have replaced videotapes and audiotapes with computer hard drives and other computer data storage systems. Computer networks linked to specialized equipment dominate modern broadcasting. This transition has forced technicians to learn computer networking and software skills.

On the Job

Audio technicians work in many areas of production and throughout the country. More work in the film industry than in any other. Sound technicians use a wide array of equipment and must be organized in running wires, setting up microphones, and ensuring all connections and pickups work as planned.

They must be good team players, able to tailor their schedules to the needs of the production for which they are working. It is not unusual for working audio technicians to have to put in long hours on holidays and weekends.

Audio technicians working in radio and television also may face long hours to meet the demands of perpetual broadcasting. Technicians working for broadcasters will gain experience monitoring signal quality and adjusting electronic and other devices to optimize it. Other employers of audio technicians include schools and non-media industries that create training materials and the like for internal use.

Good communication skills are essential in this field, and it is probably best not to be too thin-skinned. Emotions may flare during productions, but when a well-done job is finished everyone shares in the satisfaction— and monetary reward!

Keys to Success

To succeed as an audio technician, it helps to have
- an interest in all things audio-related, from CDs to the way sound is recorded for movies and television
- a knack for electronics, mechanical systems, and devices
- ability to work well with your hands
- stamina to work long hours
- patience and determination to produce the best product possible

Do You Have What It Takes?

Anyone can make video and audio recordings, but doing the job well requires a combination of creativity and technical know-how. A professional recording engineer described it as needing to know the tech stuff so well that you never have to think about it. Then you can focus on creativity and making great, not just good, recordings. Just "messing around" with recording equipment will help develop your abilities and ideas.

Broadcast and sound engineering technicians and radio operators must have manual dexterity and an aptitude for working with electrical, electronic, and mechanical systems and equipment. However, it's equally important to have a diploma or certificate in recording engineering, audiovisual technology, or something similar to break into this career.

To make it as an audio tech, you need to be a go-getter who will take advantage of all opportunities to learn on the job and demonstrate to producers and executives that you have the talent to advance.

A Typical Day at Work

If you're hired by a recording studio, you'll work with creative artists to get the sounds they want. That means you'll spend most of your time operating equipment to record and edit audio, either live or in a studio. Beginning technicians often set up microphones and run tests on equipment to make sure everything is operating correctly and recording properly. A technician often helps producers to get the right levels and tones on instruments and voices that are recorded. Sometimes, techs are called on to make quick repairs on electronics that are malfunctioning. Technicians also interact with artists. Technicians have to listen carefully to the artist so they can help create the style and feeling that the artist envisions. Interpersonal skills are vital to help things run smoothly, especially as a recording session can stretch on for hours.

If you manage to land a job with a movie studio, you may spend your day running dubbing machines to match edited dialogue, music, and sound effects to a video or movie recording. Those who work in broadcasting may start the day with a production planning meeting, in which they learn what studio facilities need to be reserved, what equipment is required, and what, if any travel is necessary. Broadcast audio techs check electronic broadcasting equipment and take care of some repairs. They also monitor and log outgoing signals; operate transmitters; set up, adjust, and service; and regulate fidelity, brightness, contrast, volume, and sound quality of broadcasts.

In a typical day, techs may be asked to duplicate audio and videocassettes from master tapes or coordinate teleconferences, including scheduling, setting up equipment, and copying handouts. On a regular basis, they also may update files of specifications and catalogues and check the stock levels of supplies.

How to Break In

Practical training will affect your future. That training could be as an un-paid apprentice—an internship or volunteer work for someone in exchange for observing and learning from that person or using their equipment. Once you think you have enough training, you'll find it easier to get hired by a small studio or station and, after getting some experience, to move on to a larger one. Larger organizations usually hire only technicians with experience, and those who have years of hands-on expertise can become supervisory technicians or chief engineers.

In the motion picture industry, people are hired as apprentice technicians and work their way up to more skilled positions. Employers in the motion picture industry usually hire experienced freelance technicians on a picture-by-picture basis. Reputation and determination are important in getting jobs.

> **"I love producing other artists. I love helping someone achieve his goals."**
> —John Cale, musician

Two-Year Training

Associate's degrees are offered in electronics technology, recording technology, audio technology, audio engineering, and music production and technology. Among the courses common to these programs are classes in computing, MIDI (Musical Instrument Digital Interface), synthesis, audio recording, audio editing/sound design, sound reinforcement, digital video production, and Web design.

What to Look For in a School

When considering a two-year school, be sure to ask these questions:

☞ Is the faculty well known in the field?

☞ Is the equipment hands-on and up to date?

☞ Is there enough to go around?

☞ Is it available nights and weekends?

☞ Do undergraduates have the same access to equipment as graduate students?

☞ Is there equipment for radio and television production as well as film?

☞ Are internships available?

The Future

During the next decade, overall employment of broadcast and sound engineering technicians is expected to grow at an average rate, according to the U.S. Bureau of Labor Statistics. As home recording software has become cheaper and simpler to use, budding audio technicians have been able to learn basic recording techniques more easily. Although some industry professionals have blamed music file-sharing for a slump in CD sales, the music industry is still thriving and audio techs will be needed to help produce future recordings. Job growth in radio and television broadcasting will be limited by consolidation of ownership of radio and television stations and labor-saving technical advances, such as computer-controlled programming and remotely controlled transmitters. However, jobs for broadcast and sound engineering technicians in the cable and pay television portion of the broadcasting industry are expected to increase as the range of products and services expands, including cable Internet access and video-on-demand. Employment in the motion picture industry also is expected to grow rapidly.

Did You Know?

According to the *Guinness Book of World Records,* the best-selling album of all time is Michael Jackson's *Thriller,* having sold more than 51 million copies worldwide.

> ## "Music is the movement of sound to reach the soul for the education of its virtue."
> —Plato, philosopher

Job Seeking Tips

Follow these suggestions and turn to Appendix A for advice on résumés and interviewing.

✔ Keep up to date on relevant technologies.

✔ Check on possible job opportunities through school employment services.

✔ Get to know potential employers and the details about their businesses.

✔ Think about what makes you a valuable addition to a studio, broadcast company, or other employer.

✔ Investigate internships that may pay little or nothing but have the potential to lead to full-time employment.

Interview with a Professional:
Q&A
David Phillippi
Sales manager, The PPS Group, Cincinnati, Ohio

Q: *How did you get started?*

A: I've had the luxury of working in several different fields during my communications career and received my first actual employment opportunity as a sophomore at Ohio University-Zanesville by networking with one of my professors who recommended me for a camera operator's position at the local cable station. By the time I graduated from school I had several different professional experiences to list on my résumé, which put me far ahead of other applicants for my first full-time job within three months of graduation.

Q: *What's a typical day like?*

A: There are always ups and downs in everything you do, but I really love my job! In the communications industry you will have to work with many people with extremely different experiences, creative ideas, and personalities. Being able to balance all of those challenges will be important to your success. I always said that I never wanted any job to feel like a job. Still today, I would do what I do without a paycheck.

Q: *What's your advice for those starting a career?*

A: Have some sense of what you want to do for a living. Communications is a very competitive field and everyone wants your job . . . every day. Be respectful. Pick the brains of the "old timers" who have been there for awhile. If you don't find some sense of satisfaction or achievement in what you do, then this career might not be for you. I was told early on that if you want to be "rich" go be a lawyer, doctor, or even a car salesman. I chose communications because I wanted to make a difference and I can tell you that my career experiences have been "richer" than anyone that I personally know.

Q: *What's the best part of being an audio technician?*

A: One of my best career memories was being one of the assistant directors of the feature film *Seabiscuit*, which was nominated for several Academy Awards in 2003.

Career Connections

For more information contact the following organizations:

National Association of Broadcasters http://www.nab.org

Society of Broadcast Engineers http://www.sbe.org

InfoComm International http://www.infocomm.org

Audio Engineering Society http://www.aes.org/

Associate's Degree Programs

Here are a few schools with well-regarded audio technician programs:

Ohio University-Zanesville, Zanesville, Ohio

Houston Community College System, Northwest College, Houston, Texas

Valencia Community College, Orlando, Florida

Shoreline Community College, Seattle, Washington

Financial Aid

Here are scholarships for those pursing an education as an audio technician. Turn to Appendix B for more on financial aid for two-year students.

AAUW Educational Foundation http://www.aauw.org

Audio Engineering Society Educational Foundation http://www.aes.org/education/edu_foundation.html

Related Careers

Engineering technician, electrical and electronics installer and repairer, and communications equipment operator.

Lighting Technician

Vital Statistics

Salary: Lighting technicians earn a median annual income of about $32,000, according to the 2006 figures from the U.S. Bureau of Labor Statistics.

Employment: Job growth for lighting technicians is projected to keep pace with the average for all occupations through 2014, according to the Bureau of Labor Statistics.

Education: In addition to courses in the principles of electricity, lighting, and theater arts, training should include work as a production assistant on college and university films or stage productions.

Work Environment: Lighting technicians work inside on stage sets and studio sound stages, as well as outside on studio lots or on location. They may have to be ready to work under all weather conditions.

Anyone who's been around a TV or theatrical production knows that before you have the camera and action, you first need lights. Lighting technicians, also known as *gaffers,* work behind the scenes on movies, television shows, rock concerts, corporate events, and stage plays. Sometimes they add realism; other times, dramatic effect. Either way, they are key players in any staged event.

Technicians interpret the ideas of lighting designers, directors, and stage managers to plan and install suitable lighting for the production's needs, overcoming any practical or technical problems.

The lighting effects technicians handle range from strobe, searchlight, and special effects lighting for outside concerts to basic stage lighting and spotlighting for a play or musical. When an actor has a dramatic monologue and needs a single spotlight, the technician assures that the light is in place and coming on at the right moment with the right intensity. The spot may gradually fade to black, all under the guidance of the trained tech.

While some lighting equipment is manipulated by hand, more sophisticated productions demand that lights turn on and off, swivel, and rise, all through the precision of computer automation. Gaffers check that power is available for lights as well as audio equipment. If a light goes out, they scramble to change the bulb.

Gaffers apply their skills in television and radio broadcasting, motion pictures, audio and video productions, theatrical and staged entertainment, and corporate presentations. When they work on movies and TV shows, lighting technicians are part of a production team that implements the director's interpretation of the script. They decide how to obtain the desired lighting effects. Their tasks include running light boards, *gelling* lights (putting colored plastic called *gels* over lights to change colors), laying wiring, and rigging lighting equipment. They often need to know how to use specialized lighting equipment such as microprocessor-based lighting control consoles. Outside performances tend to require more complex lighting than television studio performances. Film work can involve highly complex lighting designs and require many special effects.

The use of computers in filmmaking has added another dimension to the already diverse jobs of lighting technicians. Operating computerized dimmer and lighting systems are full-time jobs for many lighting technicians. Some gaffers also soar above sets in aerial lifts to light the action from very high angles.

The majority of workers in this industry are freelancers hired for specific jobs. Because virtually all film production companies and television networks employ union workers, lighting technicians usually become union members. Like many professionals in the film and TV business, many gaffers belong to the International Alliance of Theatrical Stage Employees (IATSE), the Moving Picture Technicians, the Artists and Allied Crafts, and/or the United Scenic Artists Association.

On the Job

While most lighting technicians spend a lot of time in studios, working conditions can be quite varied. Depending on the type of project and employer, a lighting tech might work in any of the following environments:

- in a TV studio, where conditions can range from cool and well-lit to stuffy and oppressive
- in a theater which may be hot and cramped or spacious and airy
- on walkways, ladders, scaffolding, or cranes
- on location in a street or open space at the mercy of the weather

Safety can be an issue for lighting technicians. More than other members of the production team, they are expected to work high above the action. Some also handle pyrotechnics, creating firework displays for rock shows and community events. They frequently wear overalls, boots, and hard hats, and carry tools for quick fixes.

Their hours of work must meet the demands of a shooting schedule or performance, and are likely to include evening and weekend work. During the day, equipment is installed and used in rehearsals. Evening shows may finish late at night, and technicians may work into the early hours of the morning to dismantle and pack up the equipment.

Touring productions and road shows travel the whole of the country and sometimes overseas. Tours may last for months, with long trips between each venue. Film and television work can be just as demanding, and technicians may travel widely, depending on the location of the shoot.

> **"Most of my images have been done in-studio, under very controlled lighting conditions. There have been a few that have been shot in nature, but even then they were shot almost exclusively at night, and again, under controlled lighting conditions."**
> —Leonard Nimoy, actor

Keys to Success

To succeed as a lighting technician, you should have

- an aptitude for electrical work and electronics
- creative flair
- initiative
- strength as a team player
- strong communication skills
- problem-solving ability
- patience
- stamina, physical agility, and comfort working at heights

Do You Have What It Takes?

To do this job requires a professional and disciplined attitude. Team skills are also important. The quality of a lighting job depends on the shared expertise of many people.

A lighting technician must respond to directions, but at the same time be creative and confident enough to interpret those directions in his or her own way. You need the technical ability to get the most out of your equipment and an artistic sense to understand how light can affect visuals and the mood of a scene. Lighting techs often have an interest in the performing arts, which gives them a better understanding of the importance of their role. In addition, the job takes perfectionism. A missed lighting cue can ruin a performance or cause expensive delays.

Finally, it's important to remember that lighting work can be physically demanding. You have to move heavy equipment around and sometimes mount it in high places.

A Typical Day at Work

The average working day for a lighting technician on a movie might begin with a meeting with the rest of the design team to review the scenes being shot that day. You've already read the script several times and also may have a lighting design mapped out. However, you'll need to be sure there haven't been any script changes and/or problems with scenes shot previously.

The lighting director gives you most of the direction you need. For each scene, you follow a light plot, a drawing that shows what type of lights are hung where, what color gels they get, how they are grouped, etc. You review the scenes you'll be working on that day and make sure you understand the plots.

Next, it's on to the set to position lights on a grid or scaffold. You've probably made a list of the lighting and filter equipment you'll need for each scene, and you start assembling it. If you're short of any special effects or rigging, you need to make arrangements to get them; and of course, you have to check that all your gear is working properly. (If any repairs are needed, you have to move fast to fix things.)

Once the equipment needed for a scene is installed, you start checking to be sure all the cables and wires are safely concealed. Besides your own safety, you have to safeguard the safety of the rest of the cast and crew.

Then, you program any consoles in use and focus the lights appropriately. This may involve frequent discussions with the head lighting technician and possibly sound technicians.

Eventually, the moment of truth arrives. As the cast assembles, you start making last-minute adjustment. (Is the spot on Julia Roberts too strong?) Then, you hear the director: "Lights, camera, action!"

As you observe the filming, you make mental notes about what could be improved. If there's another take, you may make further adjustments. You'll probably light several scenes on this same set in the course of the day. Then, eventually, it's a wrap. You de-rig all your equipment, check to be sure it is packed securely, and transport it to the storage area.

How to Break In

Formal training in lighting design is increasingly the usual method of entry. After getting their degrees many graduates start out as general electricians and become lighting technicians once they are skilled in their trade. Relevant work experience, whether paid or volunteer, is a definite advantage. This could include helping out with local amateur theater companies or on college productions. Many lighting technicians start in local theater or on small, independent movie productions to get experience working with actors, directors, and other technical workers. Others breaking into the field find lighting assistant positions for special events, road shows, and rock concerts.

Two-Year Training

To obtain your associate's degree, you may choose to major in design and visual communications, film production, interior design, theater arts, or theater design and stagecraft. Some two-year schools offer theater technician apprenticeship programs that combine classroom study with hands-on work. These programs give a broad background in scenery, rigging, costumes, box office management, marketing, and lighting.

What to Look For in a School

When considering a two-year school, be sure to ask these questions:

☞ Is the program competitive?

☞ Is the equipment up to date?

☞ Will I get experience on real theater and movie productions?

☞ Are the studios and labs comfortable and well equipped?

☞ Is there equipment for television production as well as film?

☞ Will the college help you find work after graduation?

☞ What are recent grads doing now?

The Future

The U.S. Bureau of Labor Statistics projects that employment opportunities will be strong for movie and theater technicians over the next several years. Opportunities are expected to be available in stage, film, and television productions—especially for cable TV programming. Trade shows continue to be big business and lighting technicians may find employment at these events as well as corporate-sponsored demonstrations. In all theatrical fields, lighting is increasingly being taken over by specialist companies who employ freelance electricians on a contract basis.

Did You Know?

The world's largest light bulb is 13 feet tall, weighs eight tons, and is illuminated at night. Where is it? At Menlo Park, New Jersey, on the spot where Thomas Edison invented the light bulb.

Interview with a Professional:
Q&A
Geronimo Guzman
Lighting technician, Stage & Screen Company
Productions, Long Beach, California

Q: *How did you get started?*

A: I actually started getting involved in theater in high school when I was injured and couldn't play soccer anymore. While I was working on a school play, one of my teachers sent me to observe a play at another school and saw how much better their production was because of the way they used lighting and sets. When I got to college, I started volunteering. Eventually, I got paying jobs doing load-ins and load-outs. This led to jobs as stage manager.

Q: *What's a typical day like?*

A: There isn't one. However, there is a certain pattern to each week. It starts with the weekend, when I get a call telling me what jobs I'm assigned to. Most of my jobs are at the Walsh and Orpheum theaters. I start by unloading the truck that has delivered the lights. The lighting designer will have created a light plot, and all the locations where the lights go will have been marked. All I have to do is install the right light in the right position. If any are defective, I simply swap them out. During the show, I get to hang out with the performers. They could be unknown Indian musicians or the cast of *American Idol*. When the show's over, I take the lights down and load them back in the truck. Since each assignment is supposed to last four hours, I always hope I may get to the beach in the afternoon. However, that's pretty rare. Usually, something unexpected comes up on my show or at another site. I carry a pager and can get called away from dates and even holiday dinners. I've even ended up working until 1 or 2 a.m. and sleeping in my car so I could be on time the next morning.

Q: *What's your advice for those starting a career?*

A: To do this job, you need to be clear-headed and be willing to take direction. It's important to show interest and put a lot of effort into your work. It you're enthusiastic, coworkers are more likely to recommend you for other assignments. It's also important to be nice to all your colleagues because you never know who can help you in your career. The theater community is a small family, and everybody knows everybody.

Q: *What's the best part of being an audio technician?*

A: I like the excitement. The work can be very challenging and sometimes a little dangerous. It's also quite varied and pretty hectic most of the time. Plus, I sometimes get to meet a celebrity or two.

Job Seeking Tips

Follow these suggestions and then turn to Appendix A for help with résumés and interviewing.

✔ Get involved in media-related activities on campus.

✔ Research the sector of the theatrical industry (movies, TV, stage) that interests you.

✔ Join professional organizations and network at events.

✔ Take photos or video of your work to present in a portfolio.

✔ Make a list of projects you've worked on for your résumé.

Career Connections

For more information contact the following organizations:

Studio Electrical Lighting Technicians http://www.iatse728.org

International Alliance of Theatrical Stage Employees http://www.iatse-intl.org

United States Institute for Theatre Technology http://www.usitt.org

International Association of Lighting Management Companies http://www.nalmco.org

Associate's Degree Programs

Here are a few schools with two-year programs related to theater and movie production, including training in lighting:

Los Angeles City College, Los Angeles, California

Art Institute of Pittsburgh, Pittsburgh, Pennsylvania

Guilford Technical Community College, High Point, North Carolina

Lane Community College, Eugene, Oregon

Mercer County Community College, West Windsor, New Jersey

Financial Aid

Here are scholarships for students pursuing training as a lighting technician. Turn to Appendix B for more on financial aid for two-year students.

The Lighting Practice Awards Scholarships http://livedesignonline.com

International Communications Industries Foundation Scholarship http://infocomm.org/foundation

Women in Film Foundation http://www.wif.org

National Television Academy Foundation Scholarships
http://www.emmyonline.org/emmy/academy.html

Related Careers

Lighting designer, key grip, special effects technician, chief stage electrician, stage hand, gaffer, boom operator, cable splicer, and appliance service technician.

Desktop Publisher

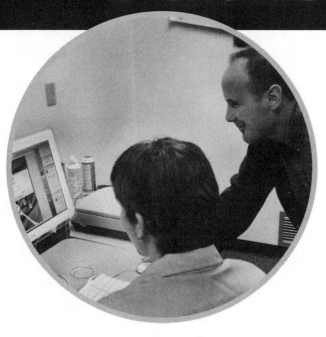

Vital Statistics

Salary: Desktop publishers earn a median annual income of $32,340, according to 2006 data from the U.S. Bureau of Labor Statistics.

Employment: Job growth for desktop publishers is projected to be faster than the average for all occupations through 2014 as new computers and software applications make more prepress work possible on office setups.

Education: An associate's degree in graphic arts, graphic communications, graphic design, or desktop publishing is recommended. Most of these educational programs teach how to use the latest desktop publishing software, and graduates of two-year programs develop skills in typography, electronic page layout, and electronic graphics.

Work Environment: Desktop publishers usually work in clean, air-conditioned offices, spending hours sitting in front of computer monitors.

Want to start your own publishing business but on a much smaller scale than say the Hearst Corporation or the New York Times Company? New software for personal computers has made it easier to design printed matter that looks as professional as the most popular magazines, newspapers, brochures, and other printed matter. Those who master the latest desktop skills can command high salaries and find many employment opportunities.

Desktop publishers use their computers to design, lay out, and produce camera-ready text for publication. They are responsible for formatting the copy and incorporating elements such as photographs, illustrations, and charts so that the material is easy to read and visually pleasing. They may also write and edit the text, create original graphics, or convert photographs and drawings into digital images.

Nearly four in ten desktop publishers work for newspaper, periodical, book, and directory publishers, while one out of four work in printing and related support activities. Desktop publishers produce books, business cards, advertisements, calendars, packaging, tickets, programs, brochures, magazines, newsletters, and newspapers. Many work independently, completing projects from their home offices.

Because some businesses now produce their own marketing, promotional, and public relations material, they hire professionals who can create these printed pieces in-house. For instance, several large financial services companies, law firms, and pharmaceutical businesses employ their own desktop publishers.

These large firms often want experts to specialize in a certain part of the publishing process. Typesetting output operators handle typesetting output devices—they load and process photosensitive material and perform routine maintenance. Pre-flight operators use computer software to confirm cost estimates, evaluate composition of orders, assess graphic images, and check fonts and other details to ensure that customers' files are complete before going to print. File preparation operators work with computers, image setters, and digital proofreaders to transfer output or data into hard copy form.

Depending on the kind of business for which they work, desktop publishers may be called publications specialists, electronic publishers, desktop publishing operators, desktop publishing editors, electronic prepress technicians, electronic publishing specialists, image designers, typographers, compositors, layout artists, and Web publication designers.

On the Job

Desktop publishing specialists work in climate-controlled open areas or cubicles at computer workstations. Normal work hours are 9 to 5, but some workers—particularly those who are self-employed—work night shifts, weekends, and holidays. Because of the nature of the work, there are good freelance or telecommuting opportunities that make working from home a practical option.

Desktop publishers often are subjected to stress and the pressures of short deadlines and tight work schedules. Like other workers who spend long hours working in front of a computer monitor, they may be susceptible to eyestrain, back discomfort, and hand and wrist problems.

There are desktop publishing jobs in companies all over the country, but job prospects are best in large metropolitan areas.

Keys to Success

To be a successful desktop publisher, you need
- ⚷ keyboarding skills
- ⚷ artistic ability
- ⚷ good eyesight, including visual acuity, depth perception, field of view, color vision, and the ability to focus quickly
- ⚷ good communication skills
- ⚷ a strong work ethic
- ⚷ some mathematical ability
- ⚷ manual dexterity
- ⚷ the ability to pay attention to detail and work independently

Do You Have What It Takes?

If you enjoy graphic design and also are tech-savvy, this is a field worth investigating. Desktop publishers rely heavily on their computers and need to be able to work with software programs such as Quark XPress, InDesign, PageMaker, and Photoshop. They also need a detailed knowledge of design requirements for print, including fonts and typography, layout, design, and possibly color separation. Sharp writing and editing skills are helpful as well.

Companies look for employees who are not just trained in these areas but who are also even-tempered and adaptable—important qualities for workers who often must meet deadlines and learn how to operate new equipment. Professionals must deal courteously with customers to take their orders and discuss client projects.

You'll find any experience that exposes you to the printing and publishing fields is useful—from producing a newsletter for your club or school to helping on the school yearbook. Try to get some hands-on practice with the different printing processes, production methods, and latest technologies.

Desktop publishers who decide to start their own operation need to be aware of basic business practices—providing cost estimates, creating budgets, invoicing, marketing, etc.

A Typical Day at Work

A typical day at most desktop publishing jobs involves many quick, creative decisions. Plus, you may be working on more than one project during the day. When starting a new assignment, you write text or design page layouts. If pages are already in layouts, you might spend part of the day editing text, creating graphics, or converting photographs and drawings into digital images. If you have an assignment that's in production, you might set type and do color separations for the printer.

On the business side, you must communicate with the clients on a regular basis, explaining to them how you're developing their materials. You also might be responsible for monitoring schedules and tracking deadlines on current projects. To gain new assignments, you have to write proposals and submit job cost estimates.

How to Break In

Workers with limited training and experience usually start out as assistants, fine-tuning their desktop publishing skills as they learn from experienced supervisors. However, an internship or part-time desktop publishing assignment while still in school will provide the experience you need to start at a more senior level.

As you gain experience, you can expect to advance to a position with greater responsibility. You may become a supervisor or manager. On the other hand, you can leap into desktop publishing by starting your own company or working as an independent consultant. If you're artistic, you may choose to continue your education and move into the field of graphic design or commercial art.

Two-Year Training

An associate's degree in graphic arts, graphic communications, graphic design, or desktop publishing can provide solid training to enter this career. Two-year degree programs give you a chance to learn the latest desktop publishing software, including PageMaker, QuarkXPress, Intro to Graphic Arts, Digital Imaging, and Imaging for Print Reproduction. Other related courses that are usually offered include typography, print media, packaging, branding and identity, Web design, and motion graphics.

What to Look For in a School

When considering a two-year school, be sure to ask these questions:

☞ Are the studios and labs well equipped and in good condition?

☞ Do computers have the latest graphic design software?

☞ Are color printers, digital cameras, and other state-of-the art equipment available for your use?

☞ How many professors teach graphic design?

☞ Have any of the professors worked as desktop publishers?

☞ From what kinds of internships will you be able to choose?

☞ Will the department help you find work after graduation?

The Future

Employment in desktop publishing is expected to continue to rise faster than the average for all occupations. Many new jobs for desktop publishers are projected to emerge in commercial printing and publishing establishments. In addition, more companies are developing in-house desktop publishing services as computers with elaborate text and graphics capabilities have become more common, more affordable, and easier to use.

Interview with a Professional:
Q&A
Nicholas Olson
Desktop publisher, Big Sky Crew, Billings, Montana

Q: *How did you get started?*

A: My first taste of desktop publishing came my senior year of high school in a graphic arts class. Although it mainly consisted of playing around with Photoshop, I did get a good look at what the field had to offer. Eventually my playing around turned a little more serious, and I went to Northwest College in Powell, Wyoming, where I graduated with an associate's degree in graphic design. I decided to attend a small school with fewer students in each class because I feel it is important to build a good student–teacher relationship.

Through internships, I was able to get a jumpstart on my career. Working as an intern allowed me to make a smooth transition from working on school assignments to handling the hustle and bustle of professional desktop publishing. Staying in touch with teachers and people I've met through internships has greatly helped my job search. It also helped to create some good recommendations that are crucial when going through the job interview process.

Q: *What's a typical day like?*

A: With deadlines constantly closing in on you, a typical day at the office usually involves a little stress, but if you use your time and energy correctly you can always feel like you've had a productive day. Being a desktop publisher can mean working and dealing with many different clients who each have their own ideas and ways of operating. I'm always trying to find ways to do my daily tasks faster while giving each assignment my full attention to produce quality work. As I'm sure is the case with any other computer-related field, it seems a day doesn't go by when I don't have to solve some sort of computer problem. Whether it's a printer error, a server not connecting, or an application itself not responding, there is usually some technical problem solving involved with desktop publishing.

Q: *What's your advice for those starting a career?*

A: For anybody out there thinking about starting a career, I recommend looking into all the various fields within desktop publishing. Since I started, I have been introduced to all that this career has to offer and the many ways a person can take it. From advertising to Web site development to typography, there are many ways a person can direct this career. Talking

(continued on next page)

(continued from previuos page)

with people already working in the profession helped to inspire me and gave me some good direction on what to do next.

Q: *What's the best part of being a desktop publisher?*

A: With this profession I have the ability to creatively express myself on a daily basis and see the results of my time and effort displayed to the public. It's a good feeling when you know, through your hard work, that a client's idea has been clearly communicated to the public.

Did You Know?

The introduction of the Apple LaserWriter, a postscript desktop printer, and Aldus PageMaker (now Adobe) kicked off the era of desktop publishing in 1985.

> ## "Imitating paper on a computer screen is like tearing the wings off a 747 and using it as a bus on the highway."
> **—Ted Nelson, information technology pioneer**

Job Seeking Tips

Follow these suggestions and then turn to Appendix A for help with résumés and interviewing.

- ✔ Create a portfolio of your work that demonstrates your versatility, creativity, and technical abilities as well as your capacity to work within time and budget constraints.
- ✔ Customize your portfolio to highlight work you have done that is similar to that of the new project.
- ✔ Become an active member of professional organizations in order to keep current and make contacts that may lead to employment opportunities.
- ✔ Attend multimedia and professional conferences and meetings to generate job leads and acquire current information about trends, tools, and techniques.
- ✔ Update and acquire new skills through enrollment in continuing education classes and through reading magazines in the field.

✔ Network with other students and faculty. Those with experience and/or training can use contacts from previous projects or professional organizations.

✔ Those without experience or training should consider interning or volunteering on a project to gain experience and build marketable skills.

✔ Use Internet resources to find out potential salaries and how well your current technical skills stack up against employers' requirements.

Career Connections

For more information contact the following organizations:

Society for Technical Communication http://www.stc.org

Graphic Communications Council http://www.makeyourmark.org

American Institute of Graphic Arts http://www.aiga.org

ACM SIGGRAPH http://www.siggraph.org

Corporate Design Foundation http://www.cdf.org

Association of Medical Illustrators http://www.ami.org

Graphic Arts Information Network http://www.gain.org

Associate's Degree Programs

Here are a few schools with two-year programs related to desktop publishing:

Manchester Community College, Manchester, Connecticut

Highland Community College, Freeport, Illinois

Montcalm Community College, Sidney, Michigan

Austin Community College, Austin, Texas

Northwest College, Powell, Wyoming

Western Iowa Community College, Sioux City, Iowa

Financial Aid

Here are a few scholarships for those pursuing an education in desktop publishing. Turn to Appendix B for more on financial aid for two-year students.

Robert P. Scripps Graphic Arts Scholarships
http://www.foundation.scripps.com/foundation/programs/
rpsgraphic/rpsgraphic.html

Society of Illustrators and Hallmark Corporate Foundation
http://www.societyillustrators.org/students/index.cms

Eduard Buss Business and Technology Scholarship
http://www.highland.cc.il.us/academics/programs/businesstech.asp

Related Careers

Graphic arts technician, graphic designer and illustrator, proofreader, clerk and editorial assistant, prepress technician and worker, public relations specialist, writer, and editor.

Video Editor

Vital Statistics

Salary: Video editors earn median annual income of $43,590, according to 2006 figures from the U.S. Bureau of Labor Statistics.

Employment: Although job growth is projected to be as fast as the average for all occupations through 2014, competition for those jobs will be intense, according to the Bureau of Labor Statistics

Education: A two-year degree that covers the basic of digital video editing techniques and technologies provides a solid educational background.

Work Environment: Film and video editors work in cutting rooms, projection rooms, and on shooting stages that usually are ventilated and well lighted. They often do not see the light of day for hours on end because editing is labor intensive and takes great attention to detail.

Anyone who's ever watched a home movie knows how boring bad videos can be. There's the five-minute long shot of scenery from a fast-moving car, or the close-up of the sleeping dog that lasts about fifty seconds too long. A good editing job actually could make those movies entertaining, highlighting the funny twitching of the dog's nose or the beautiful mountain range in the distance.

Editing brings together creativity and technical expertise to give films pacing and energy. Editing can make a commercial movie or video a big success or a flop.

When working on a film, editors want to highlight the most dramatic or entertaining parts so that the film will hold the audience's interest. They also have to control how a story unfolds and appears to the audience.

Editors need to know what the producers and directors expect of the film so that they can edit it to match the creators' vision. Before they do any editing, they study the script with the producers and directors. They learn about the story line and what scenes the director thinks are most important. In addition, they discuss any special goals the producers have for the film.

After the scenes are shot, editors watch all the footage. They use high-tech editing equipment to remove uninteresting parts of a film or video and then reassemble the best parts so that the film is entertaining and interesting.

Digital video editing is replacing traditional video editing at a rapid rate because the new technology allows companies to save time and money on their editing by doing everything via computer. Once the edits are made, film and video editors review the film and make additional edits. Editors go through the review-and-edit cycle several times until they are satisfied with the result. They also add dialogue, music, and special effects to make the film entertaining. They work closely with people who specialize in audio, visual, music, and special effects.

Film and video editors often specialize in certain areas of television or film. They may edit short commercials, music videos, or instructional films. Some specialize in creating soundtracks. They may do bigger projects such as feature-length movies or documentaries. The type of project determines the editor's work load.

The majority of film and video editors are employed on a freelance basis, working on a short-term contract basis for post-production studios, television companies, and corporate employers. More than half work in the motion picture industry. Many salaried editors are employed by independent television stations, local affiliate stations of television networks or broadcast groups, large cable and television networks, or smaller independent production companies.

Nowadays, thanks to digital technology, video editors also may work in law enforcement or for law firms, recreating crime scenes for the courts. Alternatively, they may work with a special events video company, editing wedding or birthday videos.

After 4 to 10 years of training and experience, film and video editors may become independent contractors. This status allows them to offer services on a per-job basis. They set their own fees and can command high wages if their work is very good.

Most work in large metropolitan areas. They may belong to the Motion Picture and Videotape Editors Guild of the International Alliance of Theatrical Stage Employees, while those in the television industry are affiliated with the National Association of Broadcast Employees and Technicians, the International Brotherhood of Electrical Workers, or are covered by an industrial union agreement.

On the Job

Video editors generally work as part of a production team. Although they spend some time working alone while editing, editors also work closely with the film creators and other coworkers. Their work is always done indoors, usually in clean, well-lighted studios. Because of the teamwork involved, they are often expected to share office space with coworkers.

Film and video editors work in cutting rooms and projection rooms, and on shooting stages. The newer cutting rooms usually have space for three or four editing benches, viewing machines, and film bins. Deadlines and high production costs can create considerable pressure for film editors.

The nature of video editing requires editors to use their hands to control equipment. They also must sit for long periods of time, often repeating the same movements.

The normal work week for film and video editors varies from 40 to 60 hours. They also have to abide by strict deadlines on a daily basis. Overtime is usually paid at time and a half or double time. Editors can receive up to four times their hourly rate when they work over 12 consecutive hours on weekends and holidays.

Often employment is seasonal. The peak hiring period in television runs from July through February, while employment in the motion picture industry varies considerably because of actor commitments, release dates, and weather conditions. Editors who work in educational or industrial films usually do not experience seasonal fluctuations.

> ## "A good editor is someone who knows the material and hears the story, someone who senses the material she has at her fingertips, senses what's there and what's not there, and works to extract the essence."
> —Marlene Booth, editor/filmmaker

 ## Keys to Success

For success as a video editor, it is important to have
- technical expertise
- attention to detail
- a good eye
- imagination
- creativity
- teamwork
- manual dexterity
- communication skills
- good judgment
- normal or corrected vision

A Typical Day at Work

When you get a chance to work as a video editor, you'll probably start by assisting a more experienced editor. You may be working on a movie, in broadcasting, or in the corporate world, editing conference and training videos.

The level of creative input varies according to the type of production on which you're working. You may find you can actually be more creative with corporate production than TV—trying out new ideas and experimenting with different visual devices. When working with a director, you'll have to consult with him or her continually to make sure you're achieving the director's vision.

Working on a feature-length film, a typical day might start with a screening of recent footage. Directors and coworkers give feedback in the meeting that follows so you can go back to the editing room with ideas on how to improve the film. Those starting in editing may review a film for *continuity*. Continuity means all scenes are in order and make sense. For example, a famous continuity mistake is in *Star Wars* when Han Solo is frozen. He is dressed differently when he is freed!

Some feature film editors and other professionals still use the traditional manual method of cutting film and arranging the shots into the required sequence. However, this is increasingly being replaced by the use of digital technology. Special computer software called AVID enables the high quality digitization of sound and pictures. The advantage of editing using a computer is that scenes can be moved easily—almost like cutting and pasting text in a Word document.

You begin editing by loading footage into the system and comparing it with script pages. These pages have been marked by the production assistant to indicate which shots the director prefers and which shots can be cut.

The entire process involves:

- assembling all raw footage with the camera shots either recorded or manually transferred onto high-format video tape in preparation for inputting into the computer
- inputting uncut rushes and sound, and synchronizing and storing them into files on computer
- digitally cutting the files to determine the sequence of the film
- sorting, rearranging, and creating a digital rough cut of the program using the material stored on the computer
- drawing up an edit decision list, the visual "script," and determining the exact cutting for the next and final stage of production
- re-inputting the tape to bring it to advanced, high-quality resolution
- adding special effects and grading/coloring to the finished film or program

The challenge of the job is to produce a finished product that will win over your audience and possibly leave them applauding and cheering your hard work.

Do You Have What It Takes?

Employers look for film and video editors who understand film and have a broad knowledge of film. So if you're a film buff who watches many movies a month, you actually may be getting a sense of what makes for good editing. Editors also must be open to others' suggestions and work creatively and cooperatively.

Visual understanding and attention to detail are vital qualities as well. Film and video editors should be able to see details of objects that are less than a few feet away. They should also be able to hear sounds and recognize the differences between them. Computer skills are essential, too, as so much editing is now done with a keyboard and a mouse.

> "A good editor has to have a good sense of storytelling and has to help a producer with that. It's a hard thing to learn. There used to be the position of assistant editor where one could look over the shoulder of an experienced editor and learn from them. That doesn't exist anymore. The sense that if you spend enough time practicing on the Avid will make you a good editor just doesn't happen. It's like thinking that practicing word processing will make you a good writer."
> —Juan Mandelbaum, filmmaker; owner, GeoVision

How to Break In

Film and video editors get hired mainly on the basis of their reputations. Some employers prefer applicants with one to two years of work experience. Film and video editors who do good work often are asked to work repeatedly with certain directors and producers.

To get experience, choose a school that has a film or video studio at which you can learn to create and edit short programs. In addition, participate in a film club in high school or college. During school breaks, try to get an internship with a film company or television station. Work in all of these settings is good background even when you are not involved directly in editing; and be sure to watch as many films as you can with a critical eye for how the editing made the film or video good or bad. Also, read as many novels as you can—developing a strong sense of what makes a story work is critical to this job.

Two-Year Training

Film and video editors can learn essential skills in a two-year program that focuses on digital video editing. Two-year programs emphasize learning by doing because employers look for those who have plenty of hands-on experience. Using software such as Final Cut Pro, iMovie, and Premiere, students learn how to make films and videos move smoothly. They gain an understanding of how light, color, graphics, and choreography improve the product. Some training focuses on title sequences and how to build a narrative scene. Editing is different depending on the project, so most two-year schools review the different approaches needed for commercials, feature films, music videos, educational programs, and other formats.

What to Look For in a School

When considering a two-year school, be sure to ask these questions:

☞ Will you learn about narrative film only, or can you also try documentaries and experimental films?

☞ Is the equipment up to date? Is there enough equipment for all students? Is it available nights and weekends?

☞ Is there equipment for television production as well as film?

☞ How many projects will you get the chance to produce?

☞ Will you have to fund your own projects, or does the department help out?

☞ What internship and employment opportunities are available through the school?

The Future

Nationally, the number of jobs for film and video editors is expected to grow about as fast as the average for all occupations through the year 2014. Not only is the demand for American films solid all over the world, but cable television stations are now creating their own movies. In addition, companies outside of the media industry are taking advantage of the trend toward digital editing. As the technology develops, so does the demand for qualified individuals ready to launch their digital video editing career.

However, competition for the best jobs is strong and those who succeed in landing them usually are very creative, highly motivated people who are independent and adapt rapidly to changing technologies.

Interview with a Professional:
Q&A

Kelly Johnson
Senior editor, Go Convergence, Orlando, Florida

Q: *How did you get started?*

A: I started working in the theater before I even went to college. That's where I fell in love with technology. Making the transition to video was pretty easy. After I got my degree and was trained, I started out as a media 100 editor. Eventually, I moved up to production manager. This led to editing infomercials, which I still do a lot of. However, as a senior editor at my present company, I also work on reality shows and a lot of other types of video productions.

Q: *What's a typical day like?*

A: Crazy. We try to push the envelope, and there's something new going on every day.

Q: *What's your advice for those starting a career?*

A: Do what you can to place yourself with a good company and learn from them. School's important, but there's a lot to be learned in addition to the formal courses. So you need to bang down doors and get into a good spot.

Q: *What's the best part of being a video editor?*

A: What I like best is how creative the work is. It's not a desk job, and every day is different.

Did You Know?

"Alan Smithee" is a fictional name that many directors have used when they are unhappy with the final edit. Instead of seeing the director's real name in the credits, you'll see the name "Alan Smithee." Smithee is credited for directing everything from the pilot for the television show *MacGyver* to the Whitney Houston video for "I Will Always Love You."

Job Seeking Tips

Follow these suggestions and then turn to Appendix A for help with résumés and interviewing.

✔ Register with the appropriate union.

✔ Be sure you're up to date with changes in the industry, especially new technologies.

✔ Be willing to start in a less responsible job in the industry.

✔ Be flexible about geographic location.

✔ Know what type of production you want to work on—documentary, narrative film, broadcast, music video, etc.

Career Connections

For more information contact the following organizations:

International Cinematographer's Guild http://www.cameraguild.com

National Alliance for Media Arts and Culture http://www.namac.org

Digital Video Professionals Association http://www.dvpa.com

International Alliance of Theatrical Stage Employees (IATSE) http://www.iatse-intl.org/splash.html

Motion Picture Editors Guild: Local 700 http://www.editorsguild.com

National Association of Broadcast Employees http://www.nabet.org

International Brotherhood of Electrical Workers http://www.ibew.org

Academy of Motion Picture Arts and Sciences http://www.oscars.org

National Association of Broadcasters http://www.nab.org

Associate's Degree Programs

Here are a few schools with two-year video editing programs:

Art Institute of Florida, Ft. Lauderdale, Florida

Santa Fe Community College, Santa Fe, New Mexico

Sauk Valley Community College, Dixon, Illinois

Shoreline Community College, Shoreline, Washington

Hudson Valley Community College, Troy, New York

Financial Aid

Here are a few scholarships that support the study of video editing. Turn to Appendix B for more on financial aid for two-year students.

La Raza Media Educational Fund http://www.sff.org

Eastman Scholarship Program http://www.kodak.com

NATAS Scholarship http://www.emmyonline.org

Related Careers

Broadcast and sound engineering technician; radio operator, designer, and photographer; and vision mixer.

Appendix A
Tools for Career Success

When 20-year-old Justin Schulman started job-hunting for a position as a fitness trainer—his first step toward managing a fitness facility—he didn't mess around. "I immediately opened the Yellow Pages and started calling every number listed under health and fitness, inquiring about available positions," he recalls. Schulman's energy and enterprise paid off: He wound up with interviews that led to several offers of part-time work.

Schulman's experience highlights an essential lesson for jobseekers: There are plenty of opportunities out there, but jobs won't come to you—especially the career-oriented, well-paying ones that that you'll want to stick with over time. You've got to seek them out.

Uncover Your Interests

Whether you're in high school or bringing home a full-time paycheck, the first step toward landing your ideal job is assessing your interests. You need to figure out what makes you tick. After all, there is a far greater chance that you'll enjoy and succeed in a career that taps into your passions, inclinations, and natural abilities. That's what happened with career-changer Scott Rolfe. He was already 26 when he realized he no longer wanted to work in the food industry. "I'm an avid outdoorsman," Rolfe says, "and I have an appreciation for natural resources that many people take for granted." Rolfe turned his passions into his ideal job as a forest technician.

If you have a general idea of what your interests are, you're far ahead of the game. You may know that you're cut out for a health care career, for instance, or one in business. You can use a specific volume of *Top Careers in Two Years* to discover what position to target. If you are unsure of your direction, check out the whole range of volumes to see the scope of jobs available. Ask yourself, what job or jobs would I most like to do if I *already* had the training and skills? Then remind yourself that this is what your two-year training will accomplish.

You can also use interest inventories and skills-assessment programs to further pinpoint your ideal career. Your school or public librarian or guidance counselor should be able to help you locate such assessments. Web sites such as America's Career InfoNet (http://www.acinet.org) and JobWeb (http://www.jobweb.com) also offer interest inventories. Don't forget the help advisers at any two-year college can provide to target your interests. You'll find suggestions for Web sites related to specific careers at the end of each chapter in any *Top Careers in Two Years* volume.

Unlock Your Network

The next stop toward landing the perfect job is networking. The word may make you cringe. But networking isn't about putting on a suit, walking into a roomful of strangers, and pressing your business card on everyone. Networking is simply introducing yourself and exchanging job-related and other information that may prove helpful to one or both of you. That's what Susan Tinker-Muller did. Quite a few years ago, she struck up a conversation with a fellow passenger on her commuter train. Little did she know that the natural interest she expressed in the woman's accounts payable department would lead to news about a job opening there. Tinker-Muller's networking landed her an entry-level position in accounts payable with MTV Networks. She is now the accounts payable administrator.

Tinker-Muller's experience illustrates why networking is so important. Fully 80 percent of openings are *never* advertised, and more than half of all employees land their jobs through networking, according to the U.S. Bureau of Labor Statistics. That's 8 out of 10 jobs that you'll miss if you don't get out there and talk with people. And don't think you can bypass face-to-face conversations by posting your résumé on job sites like Monster.com and Hotjobs.com and then waiting for employers to contact you. That's so mid-1990s! Back then, tens of thousands, if not millions, of job seekers diligently posted their résumés on scores of sites. Then they sat back and waited . . . and waited . . . and waited. You get the idea. Big job sites like Monster and Hotjobs have their place, of course, but relying solely on an Internet job search is about as effective as throwing your résumé into a black hole.

Begin your networking efforts by making a list of people to talk to: teachers, classmates (and their parents), anyone you've worked with, neighbors, worship acquaintances, and anyone you've interned or volunteered with. You can also expand your networking opportunities through the student sections of industry associations (listed at the end of each chapter of *Top Careers in Two Years*); attending or volunteering at industry events, association conferences, career fairs; and through job-shadowing. Keep in mind that only rarely will any of the people on your list be in a position to offer you a job. But whether they know it or not, they probably know someone who knows someone who is. That's why your networking goal is not to ask for a job but the name of someone to talk with. Even when you network with an employer, it's wise to say something like, "You may not have any positions available, but might you know someone I could talk with to find out more about what it's like to work in this field?"

Also, keep in mind that networking is a two-way street. For instance, you may be talking with someone who has a job opening that isn't appropriate for you. If you can refer someone else to the employer, either person may well be disposed to help you someday in the future.

Dial-Up Help

Call your contacts directly, rather than e-mail them. (E-mails are too easy for busy people to ignore, even if they don't mean to.) Explain that you're a recent graduate in your field; that Mr. Jones referred you; and that you're wondering if you could stop by for 10 or 15 minutes at your contact's convenience to find out a little more about how the industry works. If you leave this message as a voicemail, note that you'll call back in a few days to follow up. If you reach your contact directly, expect that they'll say they're too busy at the moment to see you. Ask, "Would you mind if I check back in a couple of weeks?" Then jot down a note in your date book or set up a reminder in your computer calendar and call back when it's time. (Repeat this above scenario as needed, until you get a meeting.)

Once you have arranged to talk with someone in person, prep yourself. Scour industry publications for insightful articles; having up-to-date knowledge about industry trends shows your networking contacts that you're dedicated and focused. Then pull together questions about specific employers and suggestions that will set you apart from the job-hunting pack in your field. The more specific your questions (for instance, about one type of certification versus another), the more likely your contact will see you as an "insider," worthy of passing along to a potential employer. At the end of any networking meeting, ask for the name of someone else who might be able to help you further target your search.

Get a Lift

When you meet with a contact in person (as well as when you run into someone fleetingly), you need an "elevator speech." This is a summary of up to two minutes that introduces who you are, as well as your experience and goals. An elevator speech should be short enough to be delivered during an elevator ride with a potential employer from the ground level to a high floor. In it, it's helpful to show that 1) you know the business involved; 2) you know the company; 3) you're qualified (give your work and educational information); and 4) you're goal-oriented, dependable, and hardworking. You'll be surprised how much information you can include in two minutes. Practice this speech in front of a mirror until you have the key points down very well. It should sound natural though, and you should come across as friendly, confident, and assertive. Remember, good eye contact needs to be part of your presentation as well as your everyday approach when meeting prospective employers or leads.

Get Your Résumé Ready

In addition to your elevator speech, another essential job-hunting tool is your résumé. Basically, a résumé is a little snapshot of you in words, reduced to one 8½ x 11-inch sheet of paper (or, at most, two sheets). You need a résumé whether you're in high school, college, or the workforce, and whether you've never held a job or have had many.

At the top of your résumé should be your heading. This is your name, address, phone numbers, and your e-mail address, which can be a sticking point. E-mail addresses such as sillygirl@yahoo.com or drinkingbuddy @hotmail.com won't score you any points. In fact they're a turn-off. So if you dreamed up your address after a night on the town, maybe it's time to upgrade. (Similarly, these days potential employers often check Myspace sites, personal blogs, and Web pages. What's posted there has been known to cost candidates a job offer.)

The first section of your résumé is a concise Job Objective (e.g., "Entry-level agribusiness sales representative seeking a position with a leading dairy cooperative"). These days, with word-processing software, it's easy and smart to adapt your job objective to the position for which you're applying. An alternative way to start a résumé, which some recruiters prefer, is to re-work the Job Objective into a Professional Summary. A Professional Summary doesn't mention the position you're seeking, but instead focuses on your job strengths (e.g., "Entry-level agribusiness sales rep; strengths include background in feed, fertilizer, and related markets and ability to contribute as a member of a sales team"). Which is better? It's your call.

The body of a résumé typically starts with your Job Experience. This is a chronological list of the positions you've held (particularly the ones that will help you land the job you want). Remember: never, never any fudging. However, it is okay to include volunteer positions and internships on the chronological list, as long as they're noted for what they are.

Next comes your Education section. Note: It's acceptable to flip the order of your Education and Job Experience sections if you're still in high school or have gone straight to college and don't have significant work experience. Summarize the major courses in your degree area, any certifications you've achieved, relevant computer knowledge, special seminars, or other school-related experience that will distinguish you. Include your grade average if it's more than 3.0. Don't worry if you haven't finished your degree. Simply write that you're currently enrolled in your program (if you are).

In addition to these elements, other sections may include professional organizations you belong to and any work-related achievements, awards, or recognition you've received. Also, you can have a section for your interests, such as playing piano or soccer (and include any notable achievements regarding your interests, for instance, placed third in Midwest Regional Piano Competition). You should also note other special abilities, such as "Fluent in French" or "Designed own Web site." These sorts of activities will reflect well on you, whether or not they are job-related.

You can either include your references or simply note, "References upon Request." Be sure to ask your references permission to use their name and alert them to the fact that they may be contacted, before you include them on your résumé. For more information on résumé writing, check out Web sites such as http://www.resume.monster.com.

Craft Your Cover Letter

When you apply for a job either online or by mail, it's appropriate to include a cover letter. A cover letter lets you convey extra information about yourself that doesn't fit or isn't always appropriate in your résumé. For instance, in a cover letter, you can and should mention the name of anyone who referred you to the job. You can go into some detail about the reason you're a great match, given the job description. You also can address any questions that might be raised in the potential employer's mind (for instance, a gap in your résumé). Don't, however, ramble on. Your cover letter should stay focused on your goal: to offer a strong, positive impression of yourself and persuade the hiring manager that you're worth an interview. Your cover letter gives you a chance to stand out from the other applicants and sell yourself. In fact, 23 percent of hiring managers say a candidate's ability to relate his or her experience to the job at hand is a top hiring consideration, according to a Careerbuilder.com survey.

You can write a positive, yet concise cover letter in three paragraphs: An introduction containing the specifics of the job you're applying for; a summary of why you're a good fit for the position and what you can do for the company; and a closing with a request for an interview, contact information, and thanks. Remember to vary the structure and tone of your cover letter. For instance, don't begin every sentence with "I."

Ace Your Interview

Preparation is the key to acing any job interview. This starts with researching the company or organization you're interviewing with. Start with the firm, group, or agency's own Web site. Explore it thoroughly; read about their products and services, their history, and sales and marketing information.

Check out their news releases, links that they provide, and read up on or Google members of the management team to get an idea of what they may be looking for in their employees.

Sites such as http://www.hoovers.com enable you to research companies across many industries. Trade publications in any industry (such as *Food Industry News, Hotel Business,* and *Hospitality Technology*) are also available online or in hard copy at many college or public libraries. Don't forget to make a phone call to contacts you have in the organization to get an even better idea of the company culture.

Preparation goes beyond research, however. It includes practicing answers to common interview questions:

☞ *Tell me about yourself* (Don't talk about your favorite bands or your personal history; give a brief summary of your background and interest in the particular job area.)

☞ *Why do you want to work here?* (Here's where your research into the company comes into play; talk about the firm's strengths and products or services.)

☞ *Why should we hire you?* (Now is your chance to sell yourself as a dependable, trustworthy, effective employee.)

☞ *Why did you leave your last job?* (This is not a talk show. Keep your answer short; never bad-mouth a previous employer. You can always say something simply such as, "It wasn't a good fit, and I was ready for other opportunities.")

Rehearse your answers, but don't try to memorize them. Responses that are natural and spontaneous come across better. Trying to memorize exactly what you want to say is likely to both trip you up and make you sound robotic.

As for the actual interview, to break the ice, offer a few pleasant remarks about the day, a photo in the interviewer's office, or something else similar. Then, once the interview gets going, listen closely and answer the questions you're asked, versus making any other point that you want to convey. If you're unsure whether your answer was adequate, simply ask, "Did that answer the question?" Show respect, good energy, and enthusiasm, and be upbeat. Employers are looking for people who are enjoyable to be around, as well as good workers. Show that you have a positive attitude and can get along well with others by not bragging during the interview, overstating your experience, or giving the appearance of being too self-absorbed. Avoid one-word answers, but at the same time don't blather. If you're faced with a silence after giving your response, pause for a few seconds, and then ask, "Is there anything else you'd like me to add?" Never look at your watch or answer your cellphone during an interview.

Near the interview's end, the interviewer is likely to ask you if you have any questions. Make sure that you have a few prepared, for instance:

☞ *"Tell me about the production process."*

☞ *"What's your biggest short-term challenge?"*

☞ *"How have recent business trends affected the company?"*

☞ *"Is there anything else that I can provide you with to help you make your decision?"*

☞ *"When will you make your hiring decision?"*

During a first interview, never ask questions like, "What's the pay?" "What are the benefits?" or "How much vacation time will I get?"

Find the Right Look

Appropriate dressing and grooming is also essential to interviewing success. For business jobs and many other occupations, it's appropriate to come to an interview in a nice (not stuffy) suit. However, different fields have various dress codes. In the music business, for instance, "business casual" reigns for many jobs. This is a slightly modified look, where slacks and a jacket are just fine for a guy, and a nice skirt and blouse and jacket or sweater are acceptable for a woman. Dressing overly "cool" will usually backfire.

In general, watch all of the basics from the shoes on up (no sneakers or sandals, and no overly high heels or short skirts for women). Also avoid attention-getting necklines, girls. Keep jewelry and other "bling" to a minimum. Tattoos and body jewelry are becoming more acceptable, but if you can take out piercings (other than in your ear), you're better off. Similarly, unusual hairstyles or colors may bias an employer against you, rightly or wrongly. Make sure your hair is neat and acceptable (get a haircut?). Also go light on the makeup, self-tanning products, body scents, and other grooming agents. Don't wear a baseball cap or any other type of hat; and by all means, take off your sunglasses!

Beyond your physical appearance, you already know to be well bathed to minimize odor (leave your home early if you tend to sweat, so you can cool off in private), make good eye contact, smile, speak clearly using proper English, use good posture (don't slouch), offer a firm handshake, and arrive within five minutes of your interview. (If you're unsure of where you're going, "Mapquest" it and consider making a dry-run to the site so you won't be late.) First impressions can make or break your interview.

Remember Follow-Up

After your interview, send a thank you note. This thoughtful gesture will separate you from most of the other candidates. It demonstrates your ability to follow through, and it catches your prospective employer's attention one more time. In a 2005 Careerbuilder.com survey, nearly 15 percent of 650 hiring managers said they wouldn't hire someone who failed to send a thank you letter after the interview. Thirty-two percent say they would still consider the candidate, but would think less of him or her.

So do you hand write or e-mail the thank you letter? The fact is that format preferences vary. One in four hiring managers prefer to receive a thank you note in e-mail form only; 19 percent want the e-mail, followed up with a hard copy; 21 percent want a typed hard-copy only; and 23 percent prefer just a handwritten note. (Try to check with an assistant on the format your potential employer prefers.) Otherwise, sending an e-mail and a handwritten copy is a safe way to proceed.

Winning an Offer

There are no sweeter words to a job hunter than, "We'd like to hire you." So naturally, when you hear them, you may be tempted to jump at the offer. *Don't.* Once an employer wants you, he or she will usually give you some time to make your decision and get any questions you may have answered. Now is the time to get specific about salary and benefits, and negotiate some of these points. If you haven't already done so, check out salary ranges for your position and area of the country on sites such as Payscale.com, Salary.com, and Salaryexpert.com (basic info is free; specific requests are not). Also, find out what sorts of benefits similar jobs offer. Then don't be afraid to negotiate in a diplomatic way. Asking for better terms is reasonable and expected. You may worry that asking the employer to bump up his offer may jeopardize your job, but handled intelligently, negotiating for yourself in fact may be a way to impress your future employer—and get a better deal for yourself.

After you've done all the hard work that successful job-hunting requires, you may be tempted to put your initiative into autodrive. However, the efforts you made to land your job-from clear communication to enthusiasm-are necessary now to pave your way to continued success. As Danielle Little, a human-resources assistant, says, "You must be enthusiastic and take the initiative. There is an urgency to prove yourself and show that you are capable of performing any and all related tasks. If your manager notices that you have potential, you will be given additional responsibilities, which will help advance your career." So do your best work on the job, and build your credibility. Your payoff will be career advancement and increased earnings.

Appendix B

Financial Aid

One major advantage of earning a two-year degree is that it is much less expensive than paying for a four-year school. Two years is naturally going to cost less than four, and two-year graduates enter the workplace and start earning a paycheck sooner than their four-year counterparts.

The latest statistics from the College Board show that average yearly total tuition and fees at a public two-year college is $2,191, compared to $5,491 at a four-year public college. That cost leaps to more than $21,000 on average for a year at a private four-year school.

With college costs relatively low, some two-year students overlook the idea of applying for financial aid at all. But the fact is, college dollars are available whether you're going to a trade school, community college, or university. About a third of all Pell Grants go to two-year public school students, and while two-year students receive a much smaller percentage of other aid programs, the funding is there for many who apply.

How Does Aid Work?

Financial aid comes in two basic forms: merit-based and need-based.

Merit-based awards are typically funds that recognize a particular talent or quality you may have, and they are given by private organizations, colleges, and the government. Merit-based awards range from scholarships for good writing to prizes for those who have shown promise in engineering. There are thousands of scholarships available for students who shine in academics, music, art, science, and more. Resources on how to get these awards are provided later in this chapter.

Need-based awards are given according to your ability to pay for college. In general, students from families that have less income and fewer assets receive more financial aid. To decide how much of this aid you qualify for, schools look at your family's income, assets, and other information regarding your finances. You provide this information on a financial aid form—usually the federal government's Free Application for Federal Student Aid (FAFSA). Based on the financial details you provide, the school of your choice calculates your Expected Family Contribution (EFC). This is the amount you are expected to pay toward your education each year.

Once your EFC is determined, a school uses this simple formula to figure out your financial aid package:

Cost of attendance at the school
- – Your EFC
- – Other outside aid (private scholarships)
- = Need

Schools put together aid packages that meet that need using loans, work-study, and grants.

Know Your School

When applying to a school, it's a good idea to find out their financial aid policy and history. Read over the school literature or contact the financial aid office and find out the following:

- ✔ *Is the school accredited?* Schools that are not accredited usually do not offer as much financial aid and are not eligible for federal programs.
- ✔ *What is the average financial aid package at the school?* The typical award size may influence your decision to apply or not.
- ✔ *What are all the types of assistance available?* Check if the school offers federal, state, private, or institutional aid.
- ✔ *What is the school's loan default rate?* The default rate is the percentage of students who took out federal student loans and failed to repay them on time. Schools that have a high default rate are often not allowed to offer certain federal aid programs.
- ✔ *What are the procedures and deadlines for submitting financial aid?* Policies can differ from school to school.
- ✔ *What is the school's definition of satisfactory academic progress?* To receive financial aid, you have to maintain your academic performance. A school may specify that you keep up at least a C+ or B average to keep getting funding.
- ✔ *What is the school's job placement rate?* The job placement rate is the percentage of students who find work in their field of study after graduating.

You'll want a school with a good placement rate so you can earn a good salary that may help you pay back any student loans you have.

Be In It to Win It

The key to getting the most financial aid possible is filling out the forms, and you have nothing to lose by applying. Most schools require that you file the FAFSA, which is *free* to submit, and you can even do it online. For more information on the FAFSA, visit the Web site at http://www.fafsa.ed.gov. If you have any trouble with the form, you can call 1-800-4-FED-AID for help.

To receive aid using the FAFSA, you must submit the form soon after January 1 prior to the start of your school year. A lot of financial aid is delivered on a first-come, first-served basis, so be sure to apply on time.

Filing for aid will require some work to gather your financial information. You'll need details regarding your assets and from your income tax forms, which include the value of all your bank accounts and investments. The form also asks if you have other siblings in college, the age of your parents, or if you have children. These factors can determine how much aid you receive.

Three to four weeks after you submit the FAFSA, you receive a document called the Student Aid Report (SAR). The SAR lists all the information you provided in the FAFSA and tells you how much you'll be expected to contribute toward school, or your Expected Family Contribution (EFC). It's important to review the information on the SAR carefully and make any corrections right away. If there are errors on this document, it can affect how much financial aid you'll receive.

The Financial Aid Package

Using information on your SAR, the school of your choice calculates your need (as described earlier) and puts together a financial aid package. Aid packages are often built with a combination of loans, grants, and work-study. You may also have won private scholarships that will help reduce your costs.

Keep in mind that aid awarded in the form of loans has to be paid back with interest just like a car loan. If you don't pay back according to agreed upon terms, you can go into *default*. Default usually occurs if you've missed payments for 180 days. Defaulted loans are often sent to collection agencies, which can charge costly fees and even take money owed out of your wages. Even worse, a defaulted loan is a strike on your credit history. If you have a negative credit history, lenders may deny you a mortgage, car loan, or other personal loan. There's also financial incentive for paying back on time—many lenders will give a 1 percent discount or more for students who make consecutive timely payments. The key is not to borrow more than you can afford. Know exactly how much your monthly payments will be on a loan when it comes due and estimate if those monthly payments will fit in your future budget. If you ever do run into trouble with loan payments, don't hesitate to contact your lender and see if you can come up with a new payment arrangement—lenders want to help you pay rather than see you go into default. If you have more than one loan, look into loan consolidation, which can lower overall monthly payments and sometimes lock in interest rates that are relatively low.

The Four Major Sources of Aid

U.S. Government Financial Aid

The federal government is the biggest source of financial aid. To find all about federal aid programs, visit http://www.studentaid.fed.gov or call 1-800-4-FED-AID with any questions. Download the free brochure *Funding Education Beyond High School*, which tells you all the details on federal programs. To get aid from federal programs you must be a regular student working toward a degree or certificate in an eligible program. You also have to have a high school diploma or equivalent, be a U.S. citizen or eligible noncitizen and have a valid Social Security number (check http://www.ssa.gov for info). If you are a male aged 18–25, you have to register for the Selective Service. (Find out more about that requirement at http://www.sss.gov or call 1-847-688-6888.) You must also certify that you are not in default on a student loan and that you will use your federal aid only for educational purposes.

Some specifics concerning federal aid programs can change a little each year, but the major programs are listed here and the fundamentals stay the same from year to year. (Note that amounts you receive generally depend on your enrollment status—whether it be full-time or part-time.)

Pell Grant

For students demonstrating significant need, this award has been ranging between $400 and $4,050. The size of a Pell grant does not depend on how much other aid you receive.

Supplemental Educational Opportunity Grant (SEOG)

Again for students with significant need, this award ranges from $100 to $4,000 a year. The size of the SEOG can be reduced according to how much other aid you receive.

Work-Study

The Federal Work-Study Program provides jobs for students showing financial need. The program encourages community service and work related to a student's course of study. You earn at least minimum wage and are paid at least once a month. Again, funds must be used for educational expenses.

Perkins Loans
With a low interest rate of 5 percent, this program lets students who can document the need borrow up to $4,000 a year.

Stafford Loans
These loans are available to all students regardless of need. However, students with need receive *subsidized* Staffords, which do not accrue interest while you're in school or in deferment. Students without need can take *unsubsidized* Staffords, which do accrue interest while you are in school or in deferment. Interest rates vary but can go no higher than 8.25 percent. Loan amounts vary too, according to what year of study you're in and whether you are financially dependent on your parents or not. Students defined as independent of their parents can borrow much more. (Students who have their own kids are also defined as independent. Check the exact qualifications for independent and dependent status on the federal government Web site http://www.studentaid.fed.gov.)

PLUS Loans
These loans for parents of dependent students are also available regardless of need. Parents with good credit can borrow up to the cost of attendance minus any other aid received. Interest rates are variable but can go no higher than 9 percent.

Tax Credits
Depending on your family income, qualified students can take federal tax deductions for education with maximums ranging from $1,500 to $2,000.

Americorps
This program provides full-time educational awards in return for community service work. You can work before, during, or after your postsecondary education and use the funds either to pay current educational expenses or to repay federal student loans. Americorps participants work assisting teachers in Head Start, helping on conservation projects, building houses for the homeless, and doing other good works. For more information, visit http://www.AmeriCorps.gov

State Financial Aid

All states offer financial aid, both merit-based and need-based. Most states use the FAFSA to determine eligibility, but you'll have to contact your state's higher education agency to find out the exact requirements. You can get contact information for your state at http://www.bcol02.ed.gov/Programs/EROD/org_list.cfm. Most of the state aid programs are available only if you study at a school in the state where you reside. Some states are very generous, especially if you're attending a state college or university. California's Cal Grant program gives needy state residents free tuition at in-state public universities.

School-Sponsored Financial Aid

The school you attend may offer its own loans, grants, and work programs. Many have academic- or talent-based scholarships for top-performing students. Some two-year programs offer cooperative education opportunities where you combine classroom study with off-campus work related to your major. The work gives you hands-on experience and some income, ranging from $2,500 to $15,000 per year depending on the program. Communicate with your school's financial aid department and make sure you're applying for the most aid you can possibly get.

Private Scholarships

While scholarships for students heading to four-year schools may be more plentiful, there are awards for the two-year students. Scholarships reward students for all sorts of talent—academic, artistic, athletic, technical, scientific, and more. You have to invest time hunting for the awards that you might qualify for. The Internet now offers many great scholarship search services. Some of the best ones are:

> The College Board (http://www.collegeboard.com/pay)
>
> FastWeb! (http://www.fastweb.monster.com)
>
> MACH25 (http://www.collegenet.com)
>
> Scholarship Research Network (http://www.srnexpress.com)
>
> SallieMae's College Answer (http://www.collegeanswer.com)

Note: Be careful of scholarship-scam services that charge a fee for finding you awards but end up giving you nothing more than a few leads that you could have gotten for free with a little research on your own. Check out the Federal Trade Commission's Project ScholarScam (http://www.ftc.gov/bcp/conline/edcams/scholarship).

In your hunt for scholarship dollars, be sure to look into local community organizations (the Elks Club, Lions Club, PTA, etc.), local corporations, employers (your employer or your parents' may offer tuition assistance), trade groups, professional associations (National Electrical Contractors Association, etc.), clubs (Boy Scouts, Girl Scouts, Distributive Education Club of America, etc.), heritage organizations (Italian, Japanese,

Chinese, and other groups related to ethnic origin), church groups, and minority assistance programs.

Once you find awards you qualify for, you have to put in the time applying. This usually means filling out an application, writing a personal statement, and gathering recommendations.

General Scholarships

A few general scholarships for students earning two-year degrees are

Coca-Cola Scholars Foundation, Inc.

Coca-Cola offers 350 thousand-dollar scholarships (http://www.coca colascholars.org) per year specifically for students attending two-year institutions.

Phi Theta Kappa (PTK)

This organization is the International Honor Society of the Two-Year College. PTK is one of the sponsors of the All-USA Academic Team program, which annually recognizes 60 outstanding two-year college students (http://scholarships.ptk.org). First, Second, and Third Teams, each consisting of 20 members, are selected. The 20 First Team members receive stipends of $2,500 each. All 60 members of the All-USA Academic Team and their colleges receive extensive national recognition through coverage in *USA TODAY*. There are other great scholarships for two-year students listed on this Web site.

Hispanic Scholarship Fund (HSF)

HSF's High School Scholarship Program (http://www.hsf.net/scholar ship/programs/hs.php) is designed to assist high school students of Hispanic heritage obtain a college degree. It is available to graduating high school seniors who plan to enroll full-time at a community college during the upcoming academic year. Award amounts range from $1,000 to $2,500.

The Military

All branches of the military offer tuition dollars in exchange for military service. You have to decide if military service is for you. The Web site http://www.myfuture.com attempts to answer any questions you might have about military service.

Lower Your Costs

In addition to getting financial aid, you can reduce college expenses by being a money-smart student. Here are some tips.

Use Your Campus

Schools offer perks that some students never take advantage of. Use the gym. Take in a school-supported concert or movie night. Attend meetings and lectures with free refreshments.

Flash Your Student ID

Students often get discounts at movies, museums, restaurants, and stores. Always be sure to ask if there is a lower price for students and carry your student ID with you at all times. You can often save 10 to 20 percent on purchases.

Budget Your Funds

Writing a budget of your income and expenses can help you be a smart spender. Track what you buy on a budget chart. This awareness will save you dollars.

Share Rides

Commuting to school or traveling back to your hometown? Check and post on student bulletin boards for ride shares.

Buy Used Books

Used textbooks can cost half as much as new. Check your campus bookstore for deals and also try http://www.eCampus.com and http://www.bookcentral.com

Put Your Credit Card in the Freezer

That's what one student did to stop overspending. You can lock your card away any way you like, just try living without the ease of credit for awhile. You'll be surprised at the savings.

A Two-Year Student's Financial Aid Package

Minnesota State Colleges and Universities provides this example of how a two-year student pays for college. Note how financial aid reduces his out-of-pocket cost to about $7,000 per year.

Jeremy's Costs for One Year

Jeremy is a freshman at a two-year college in the Minnesota. He has a sister in college, and his parents own a home but have no other significant savings. His family's income: $42,000.

College Costs for One Year

Tuition	$3,437
Fees	$388
Estimated room and board*	$7,200
Estimated living expenses**	$6,116
Total cost of attendance	*$17,141*

Jeremy's Financial Aid

Federal grants (does not require payment)	$2,800
Minnesota grant (does not require payment)	$676
Work-study earnings	$4,000
Student loan (requires repayment)	$2,625
Total financial aid	*$10,101*
Total cost to Jeremy's family	*$7,040*

 * Estimated cost reflecting apartment rent rate and food costs. The estimates are used to calculate the financial aid. If a student lives at home with his or her parents, the actual cost could be much less, although the financial aid amounts may remain the same.

** This is an estimate of expenses including transportation, books, clothing, and social activities.

Index

127